AF575403

SOMETHING
FOR
LOVERS

GENIEVE FIGGIS

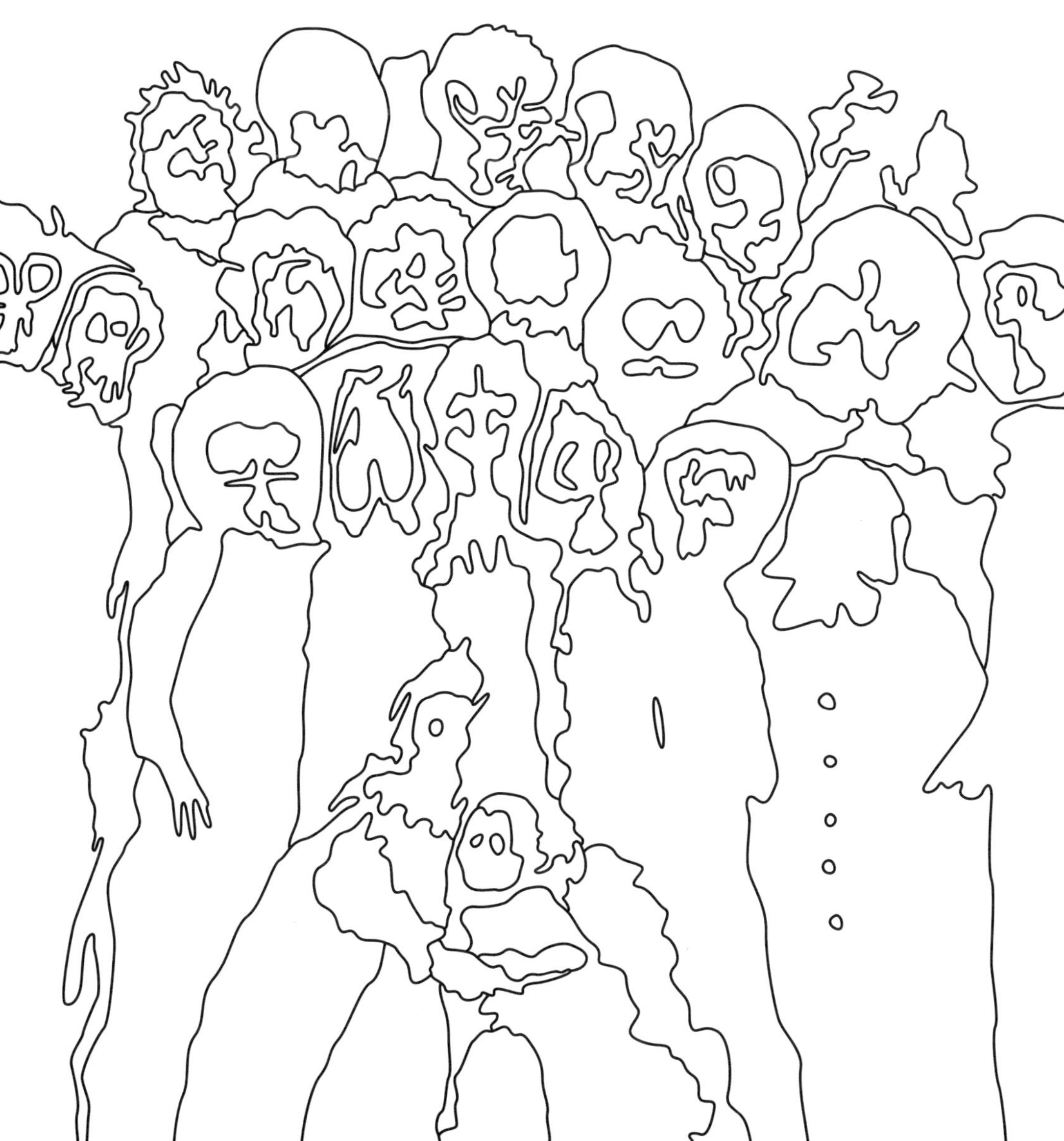

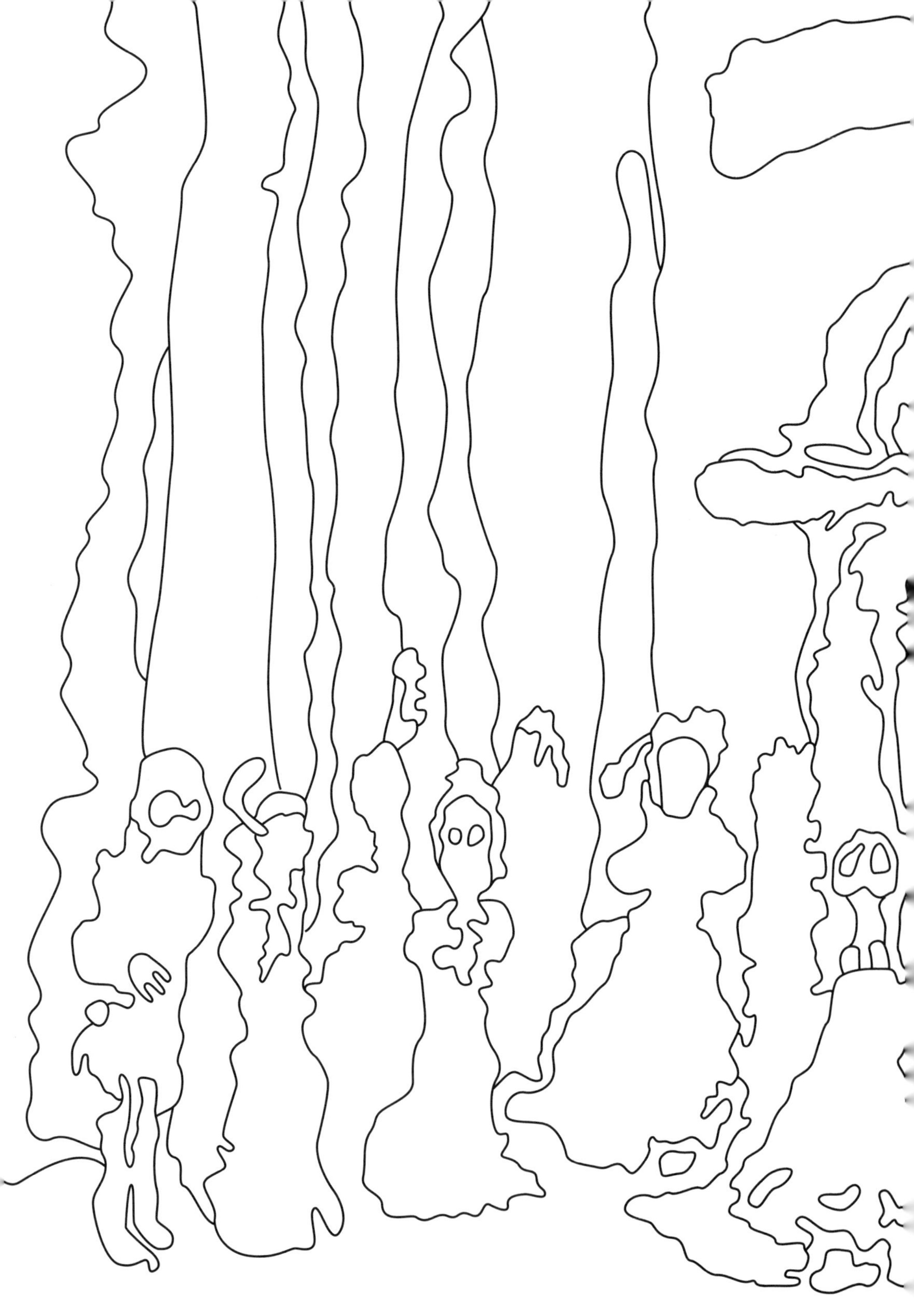

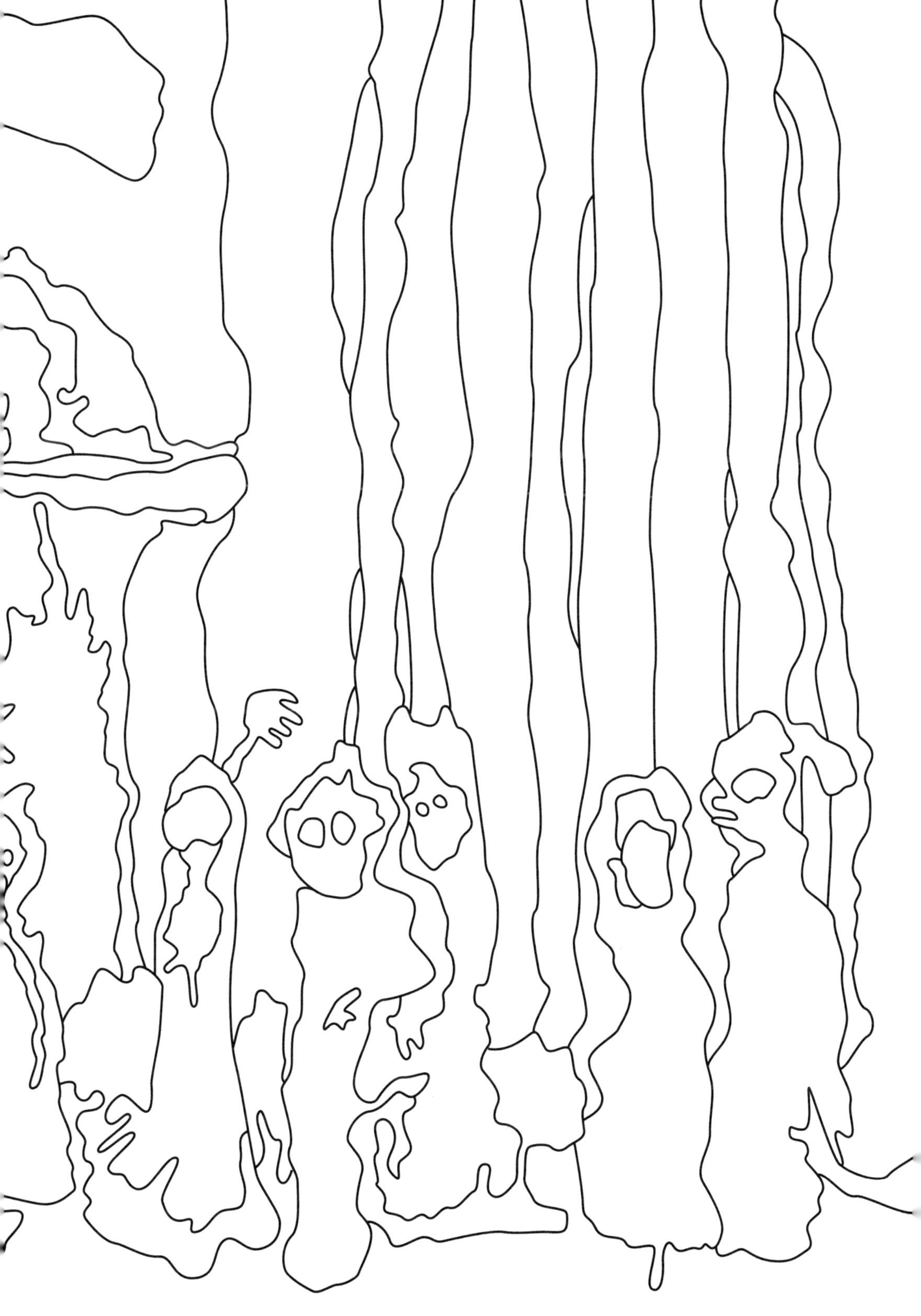

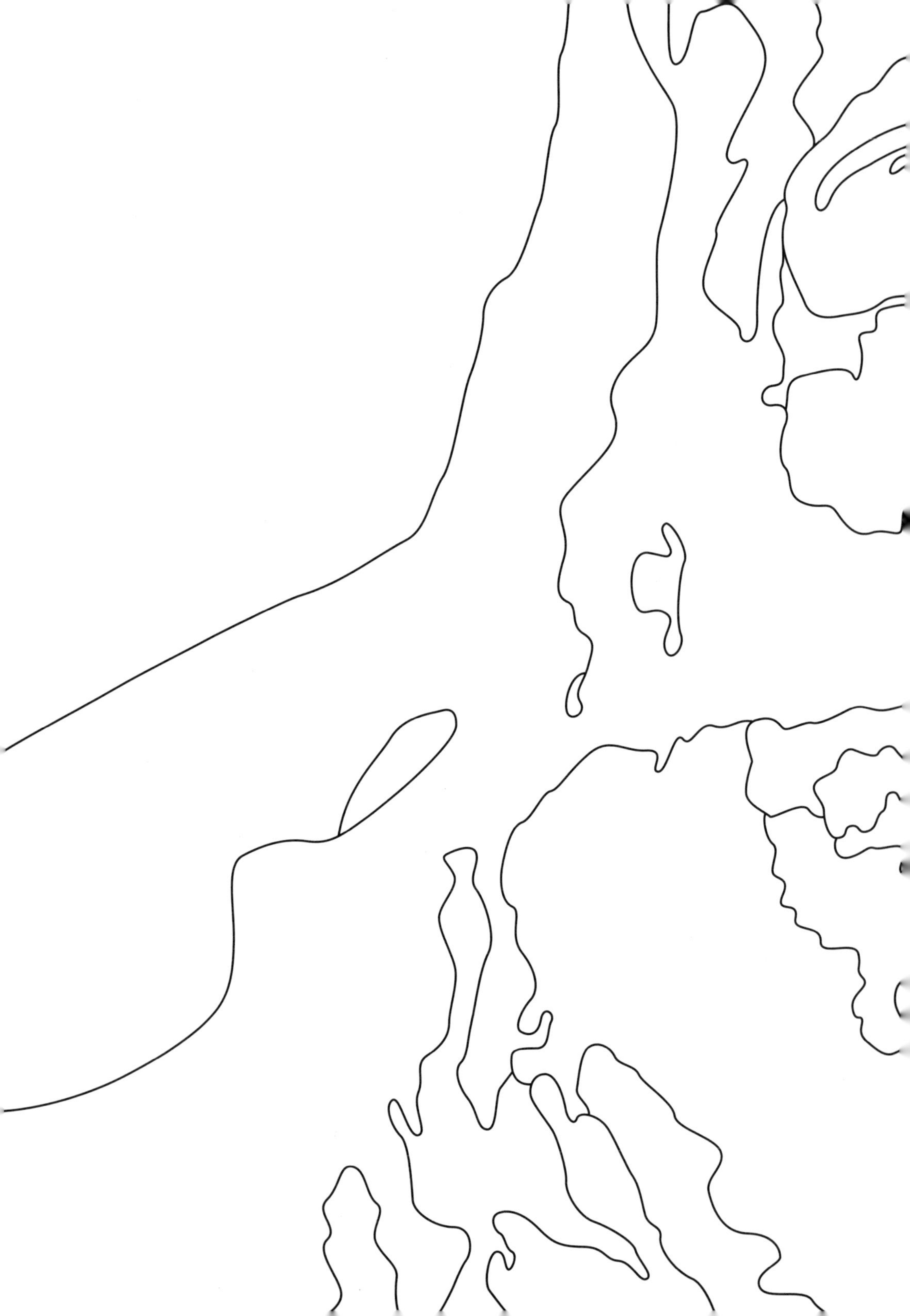

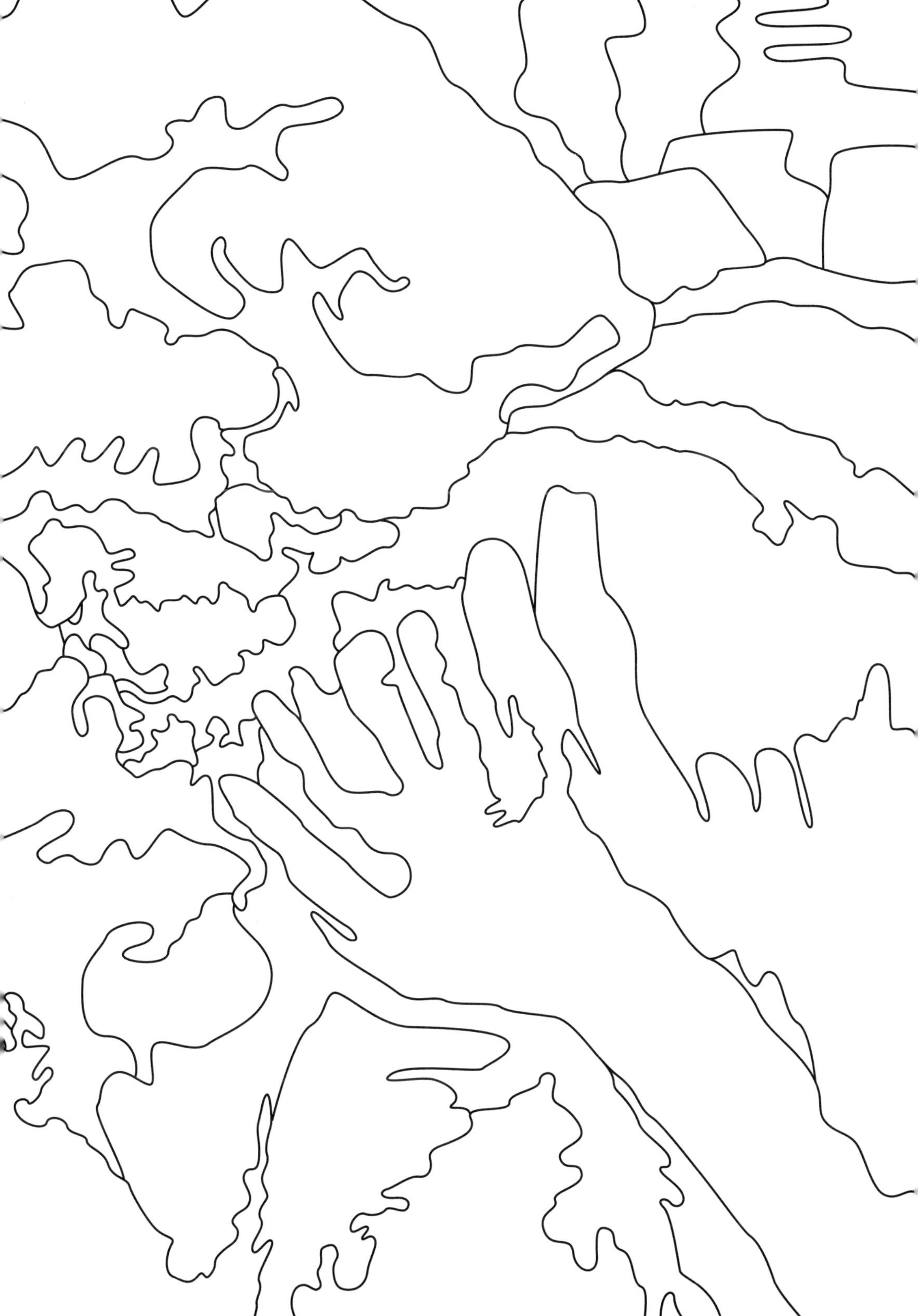

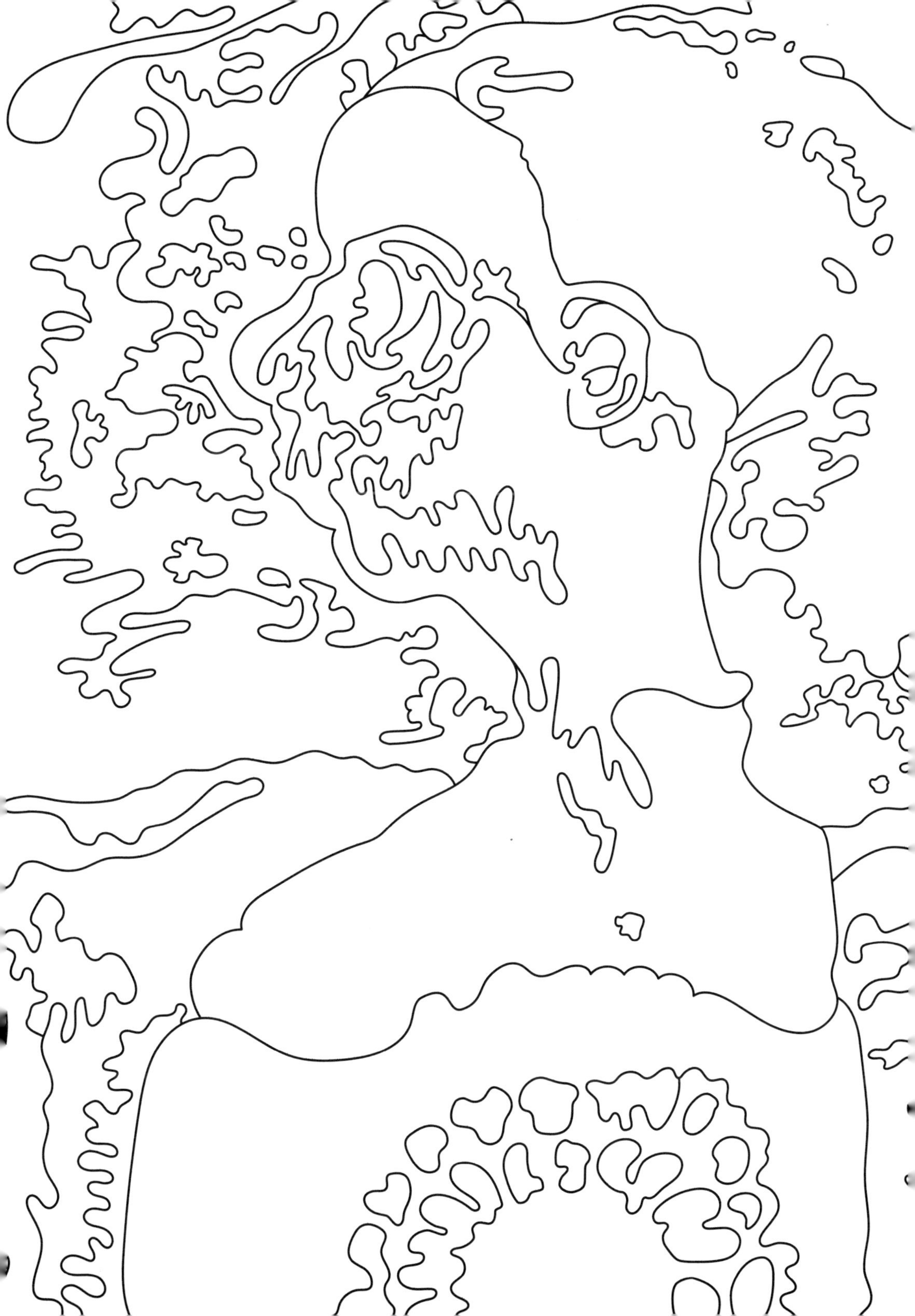

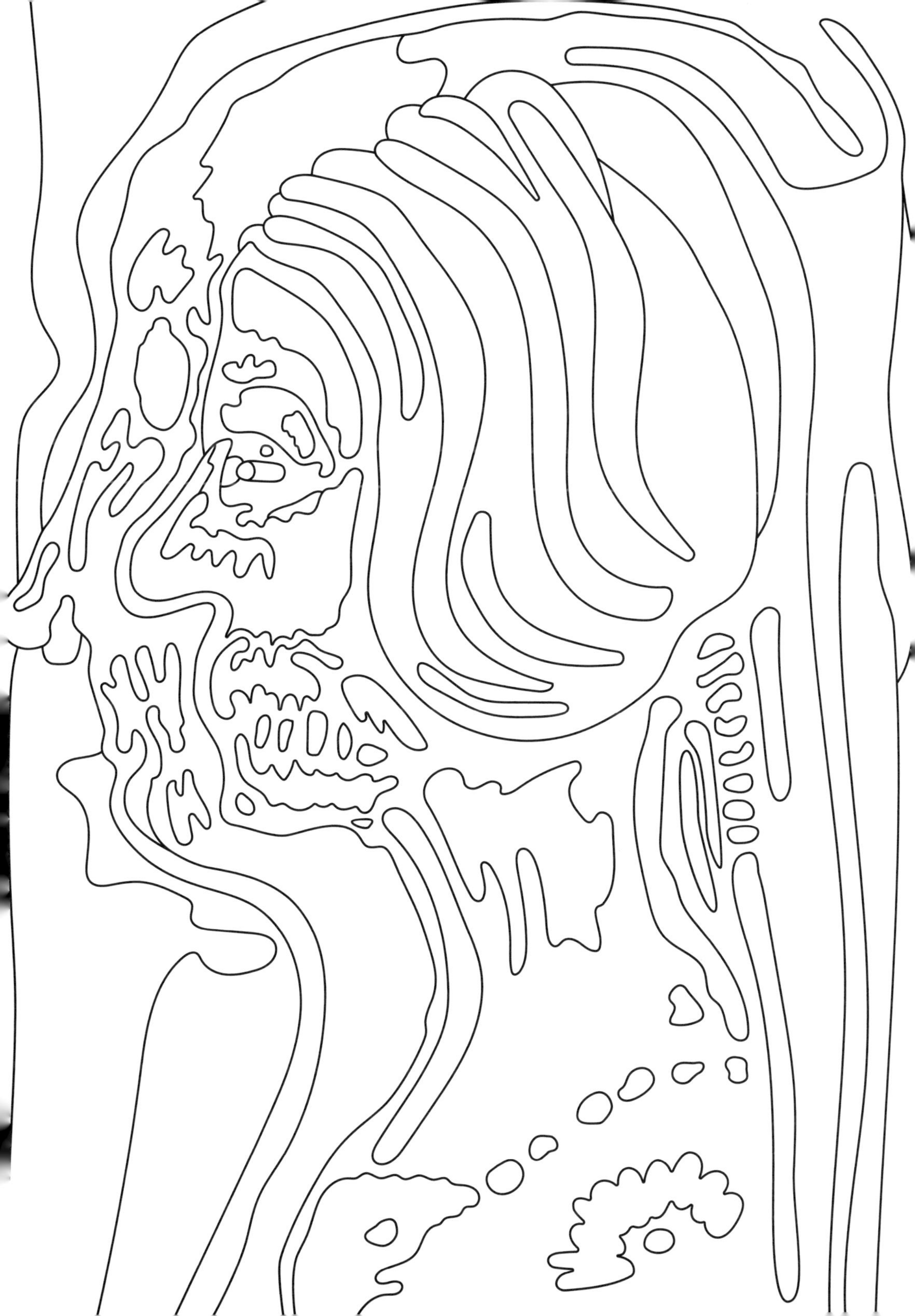

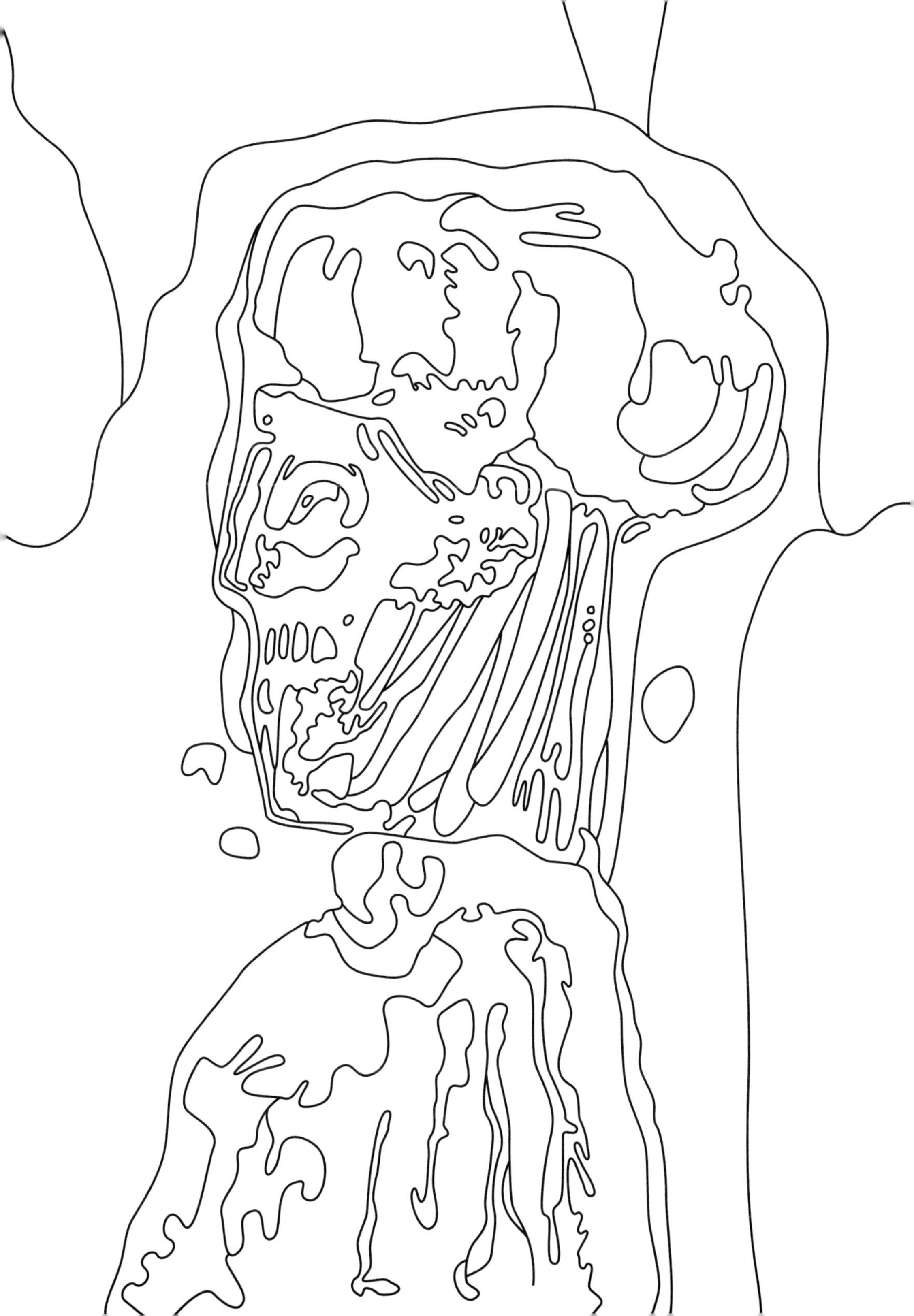

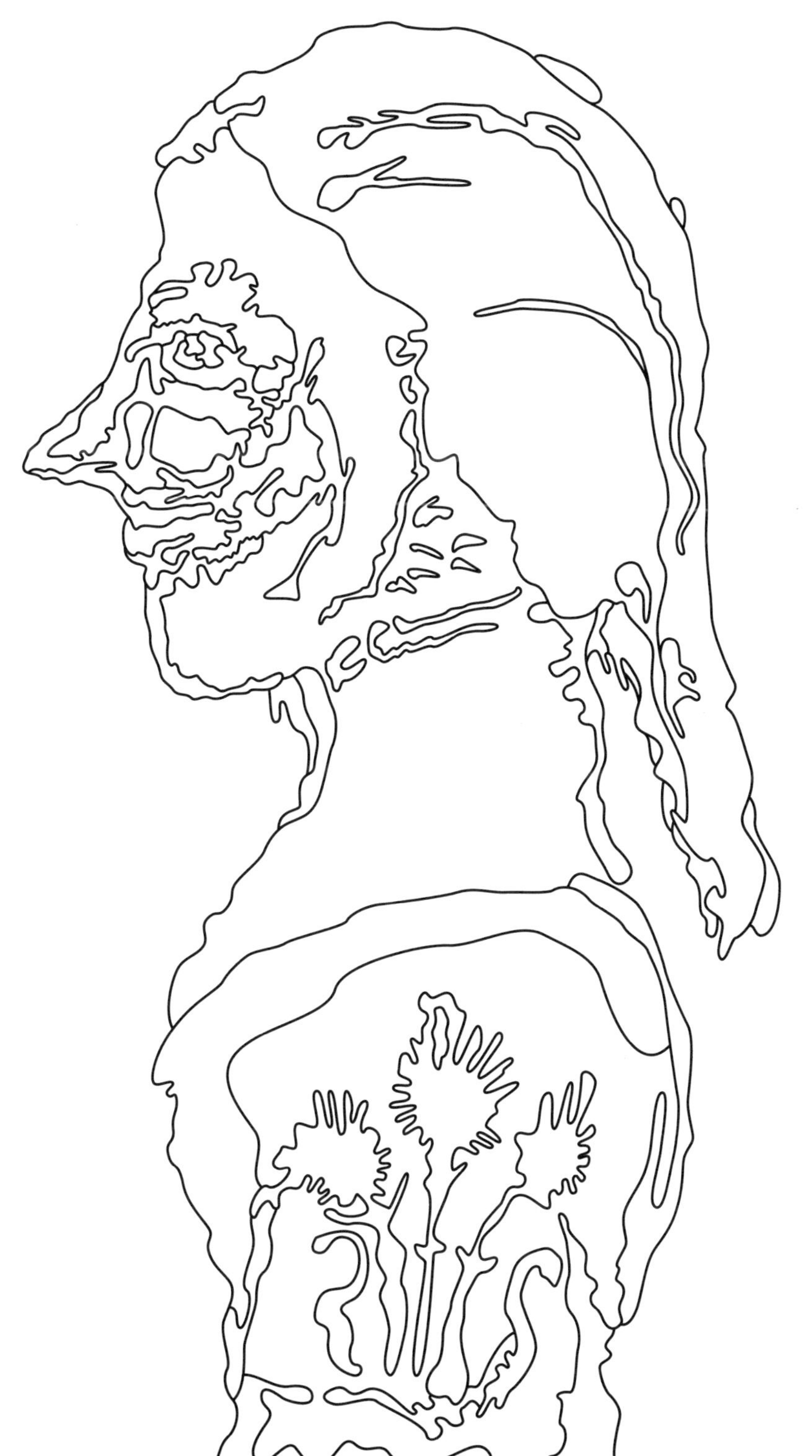

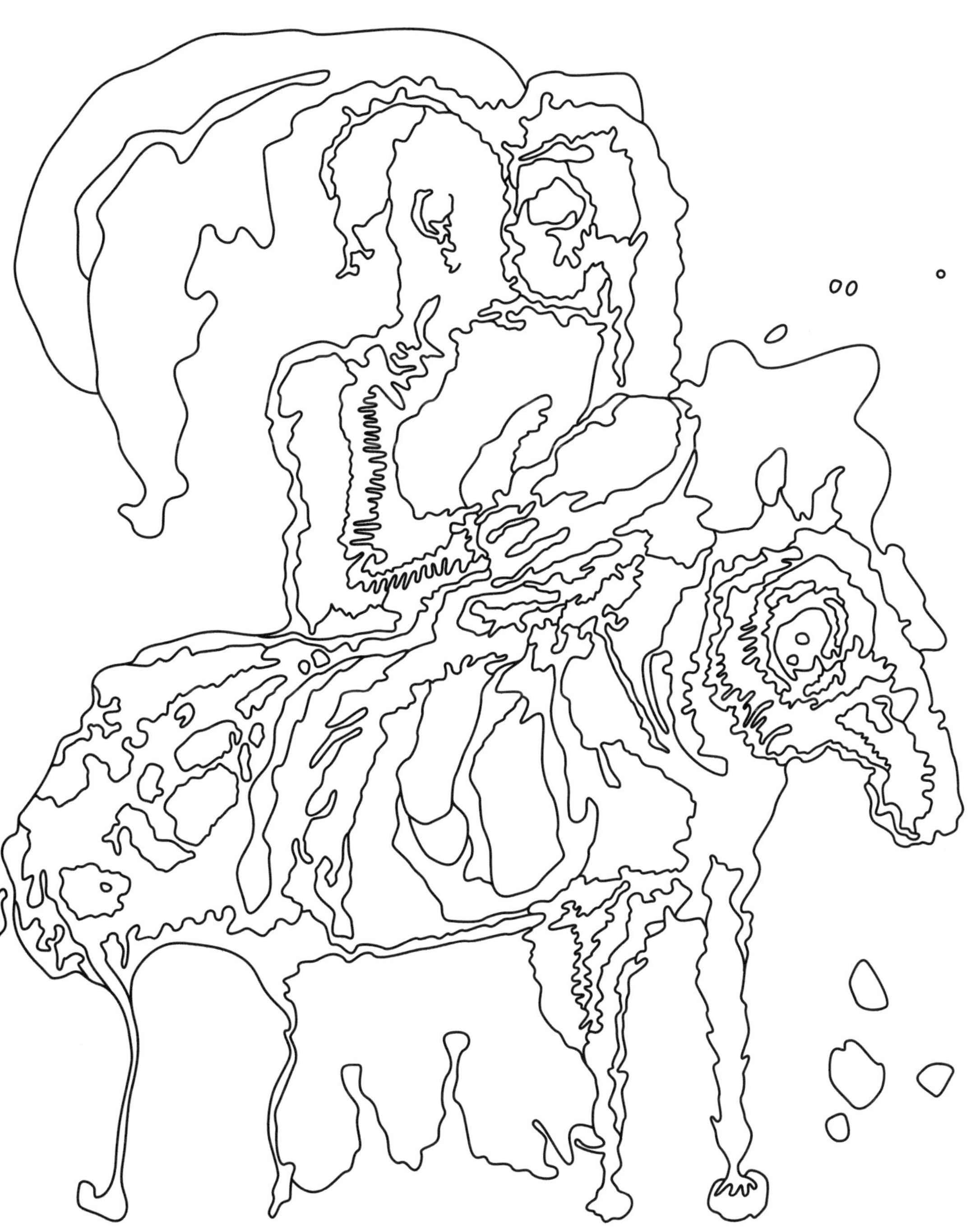

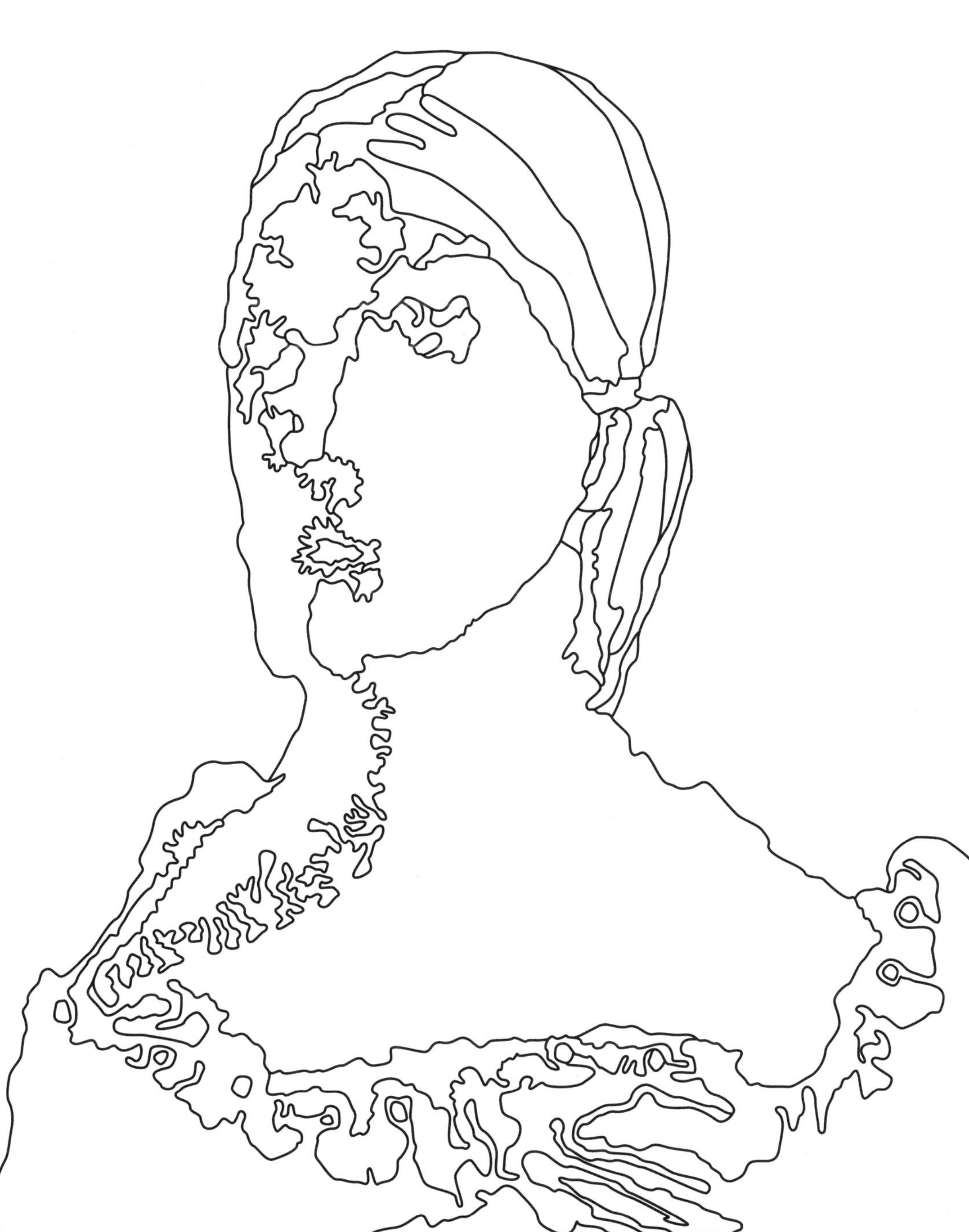

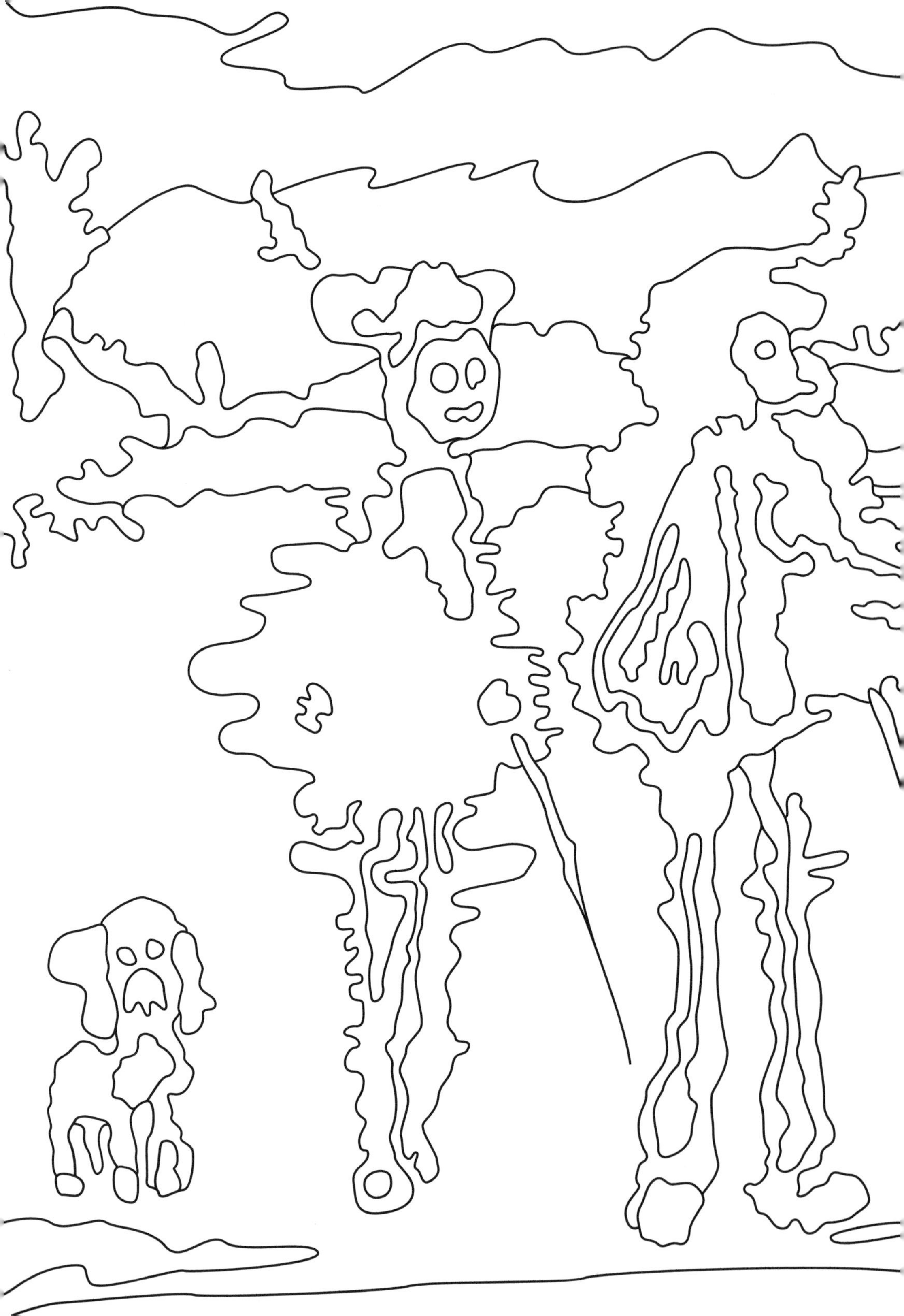

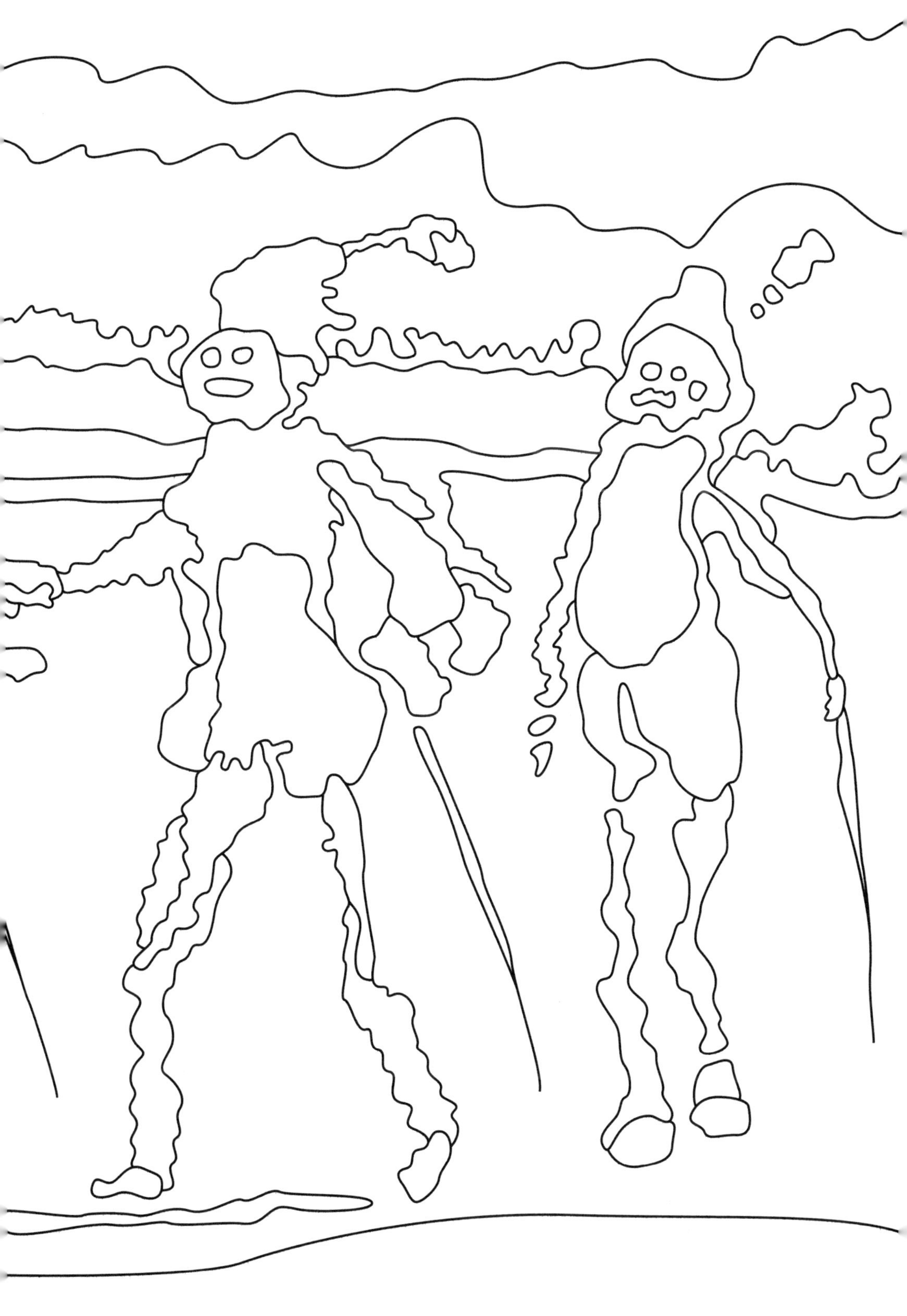

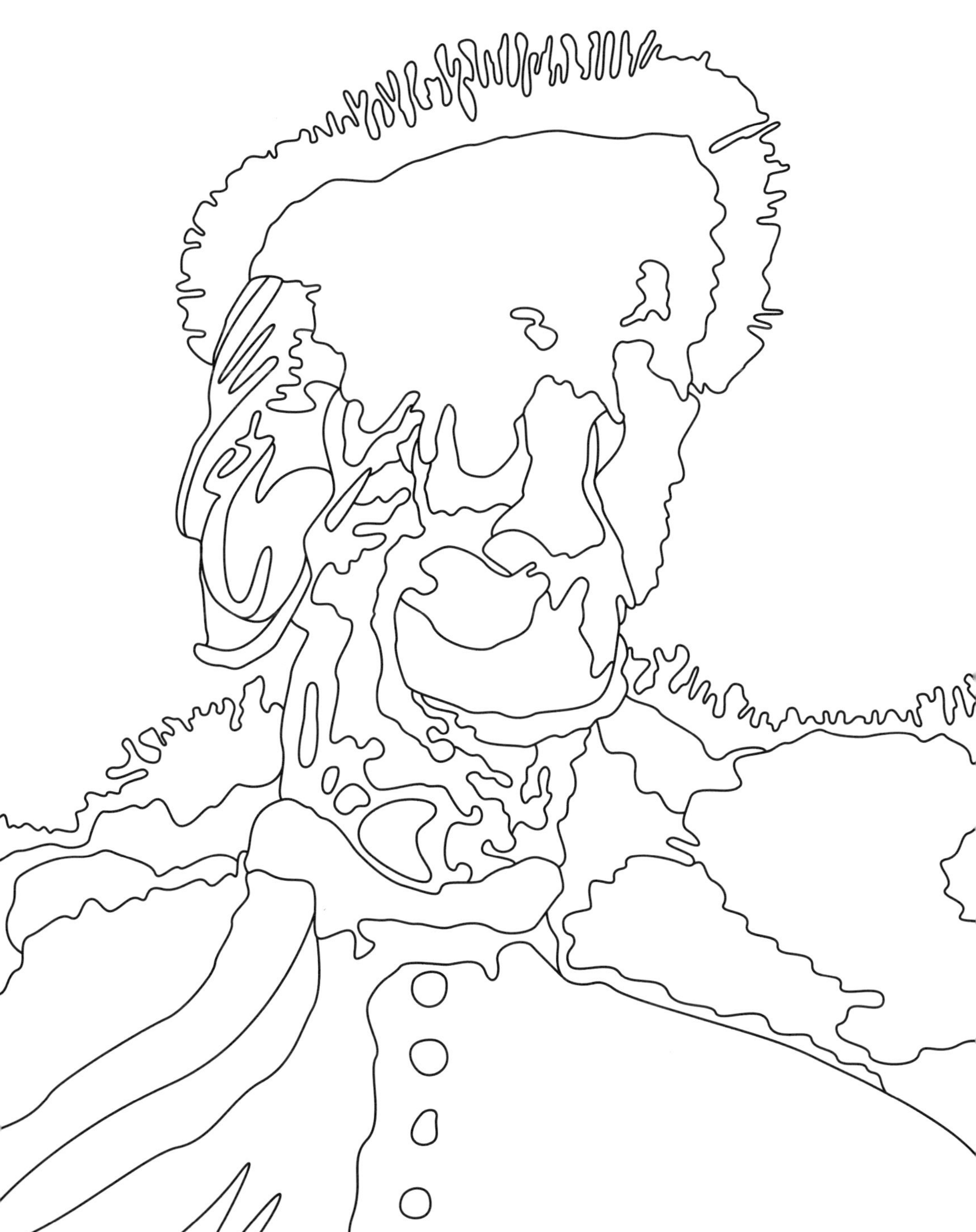

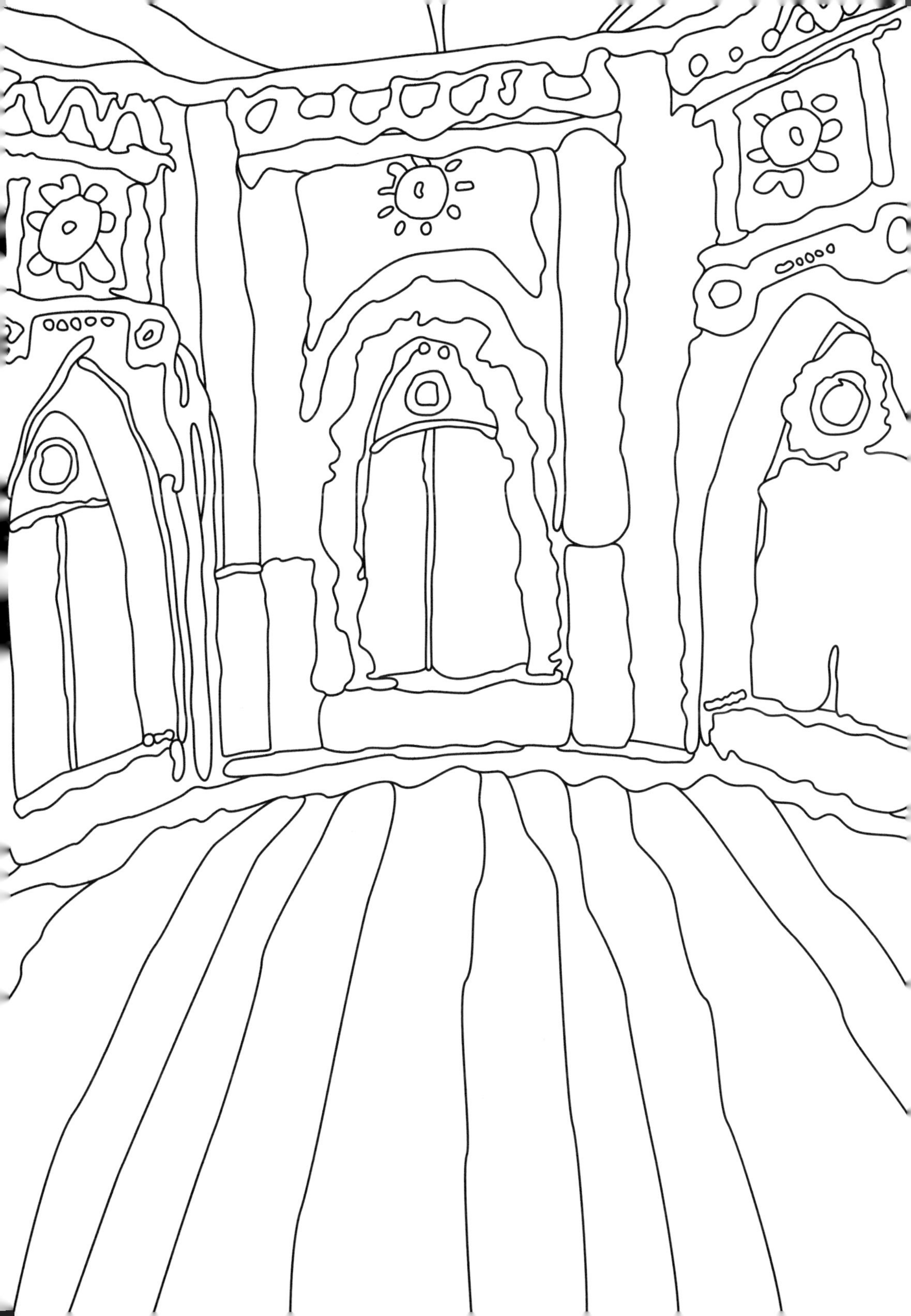

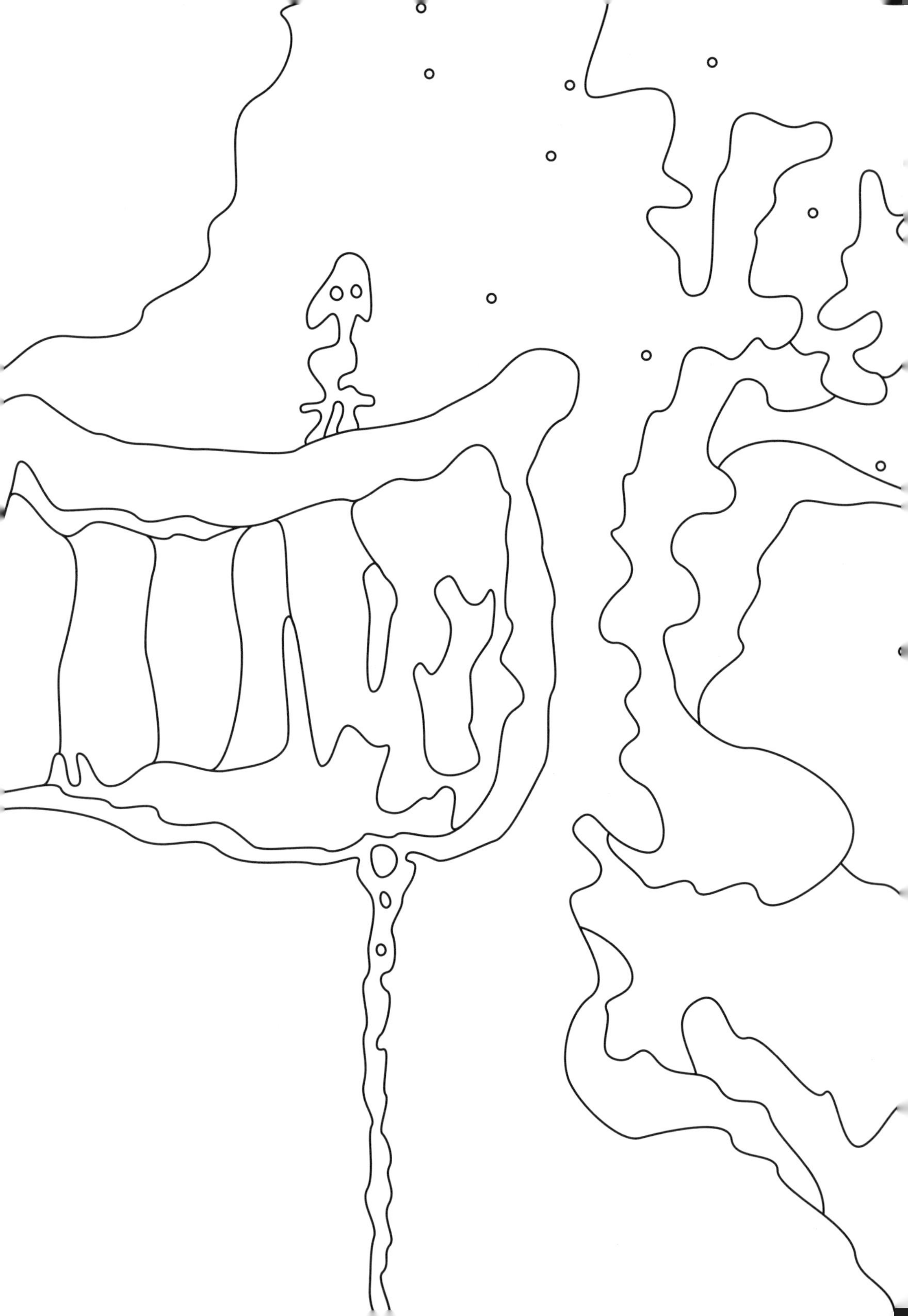

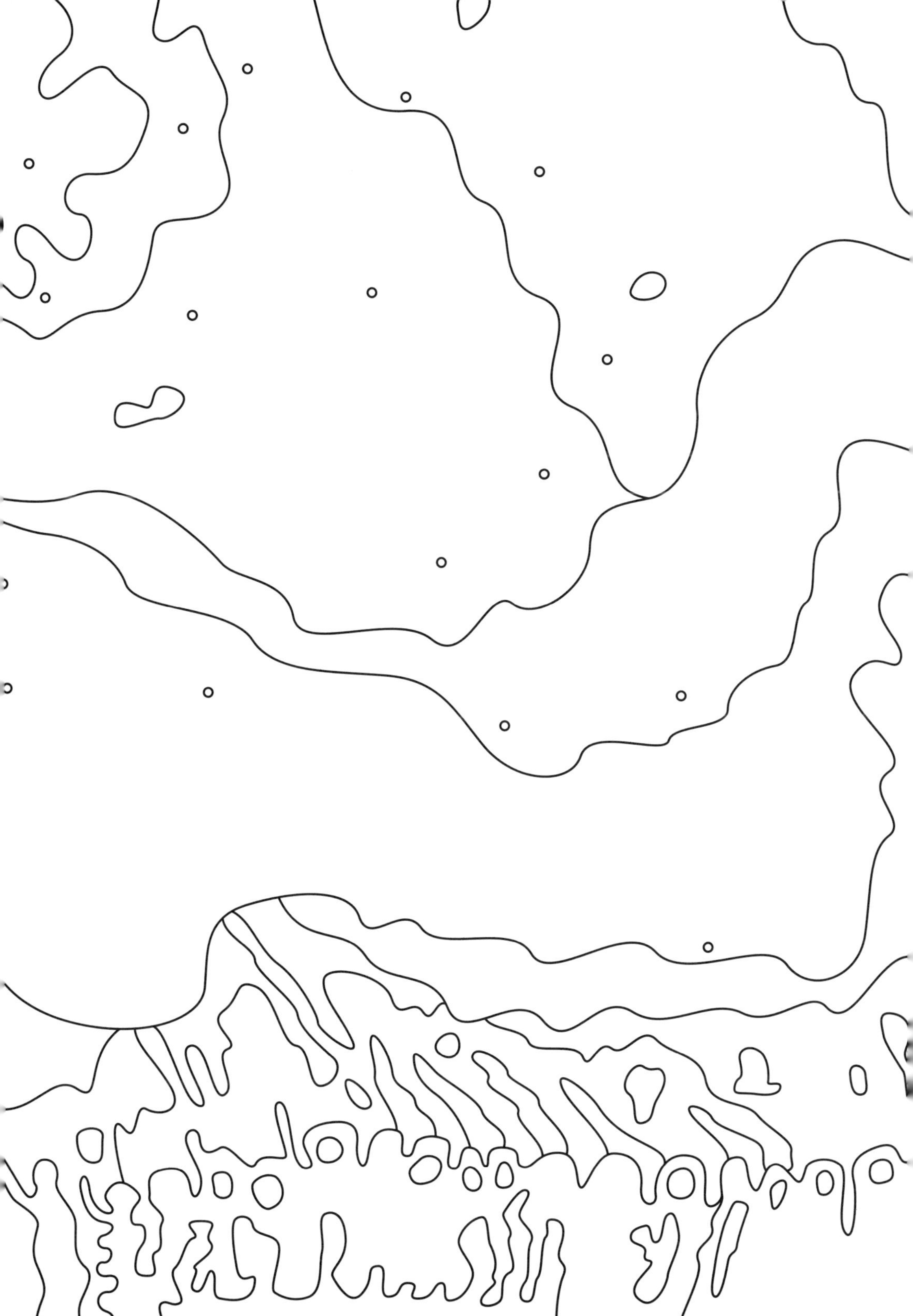

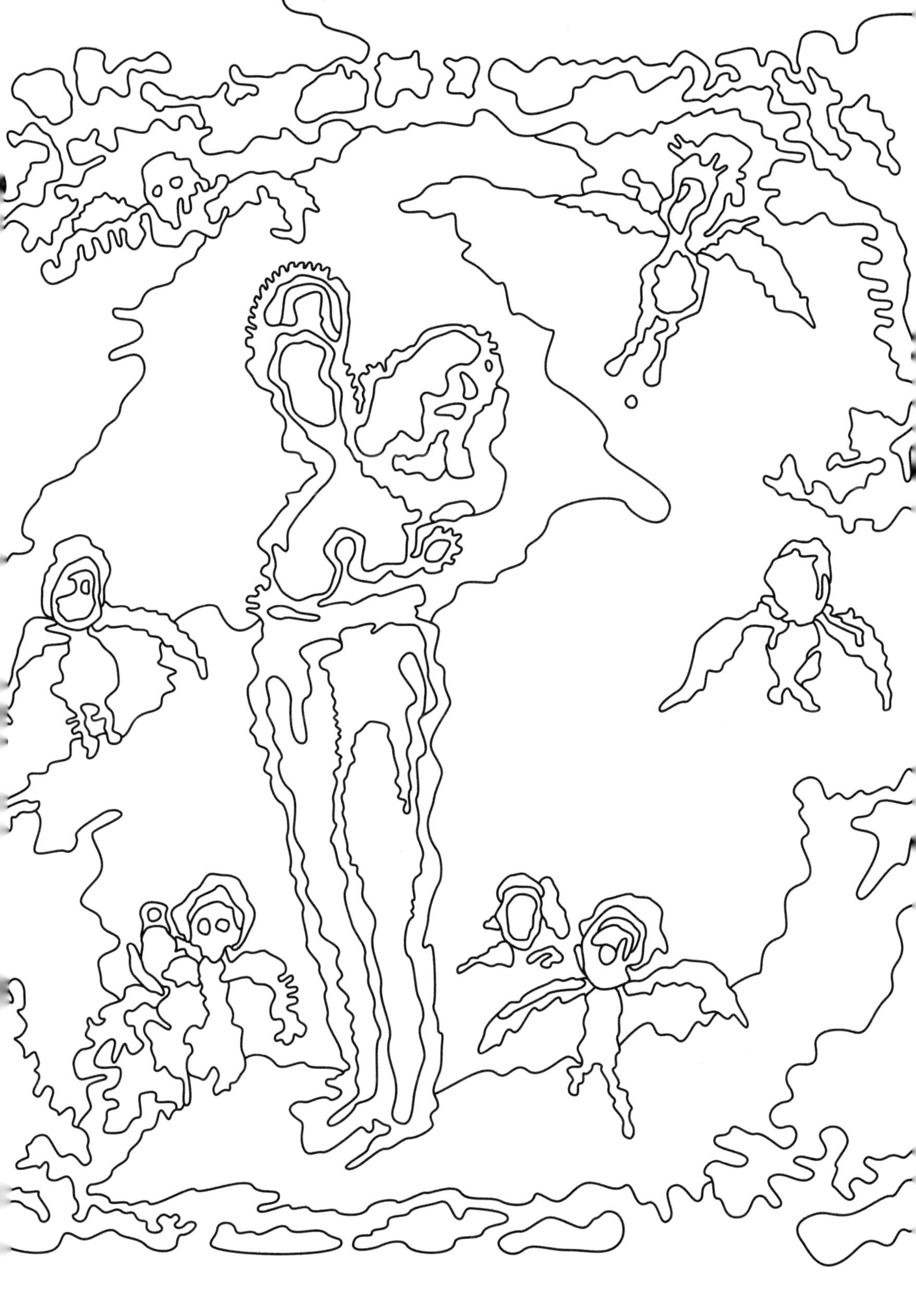

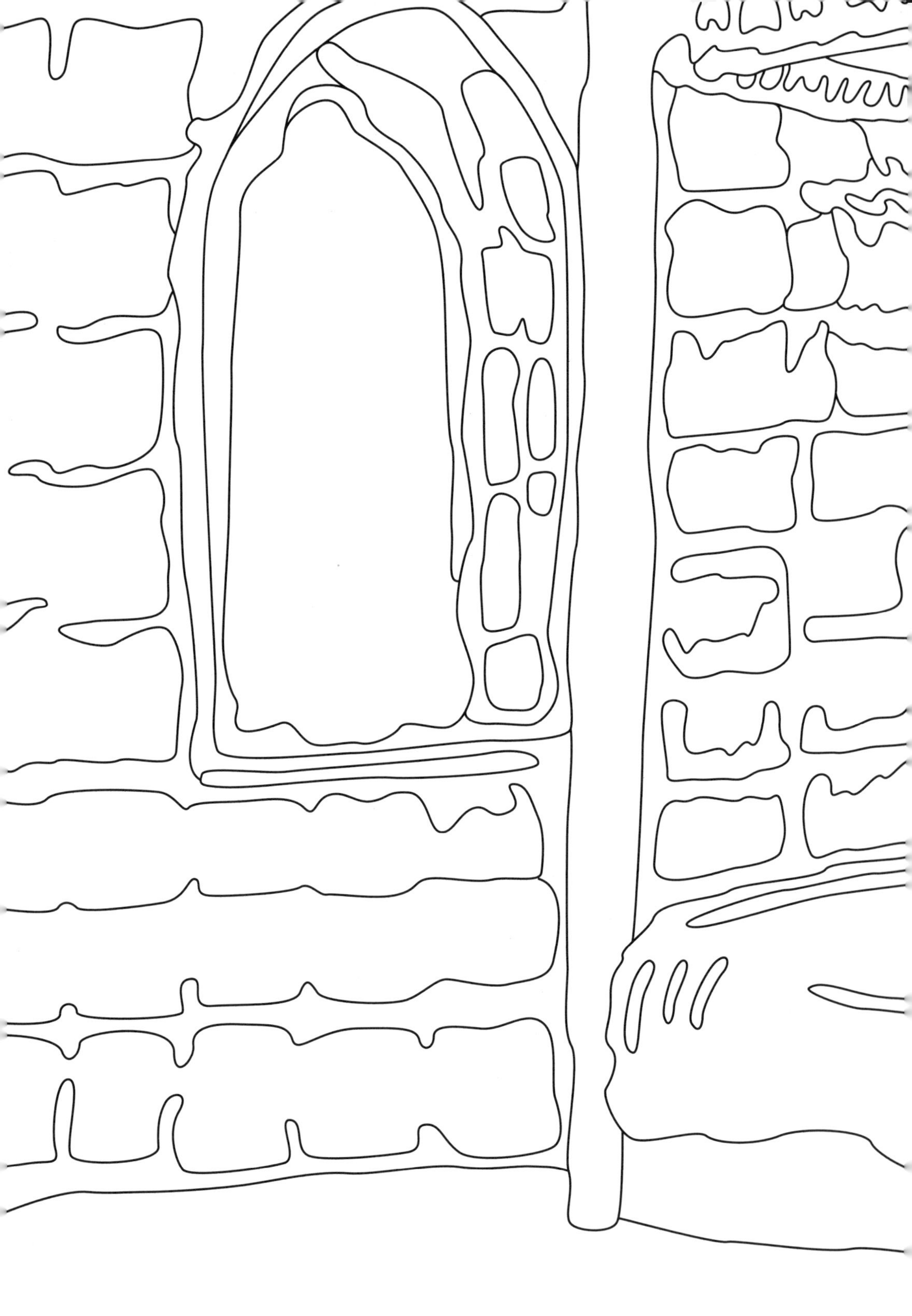

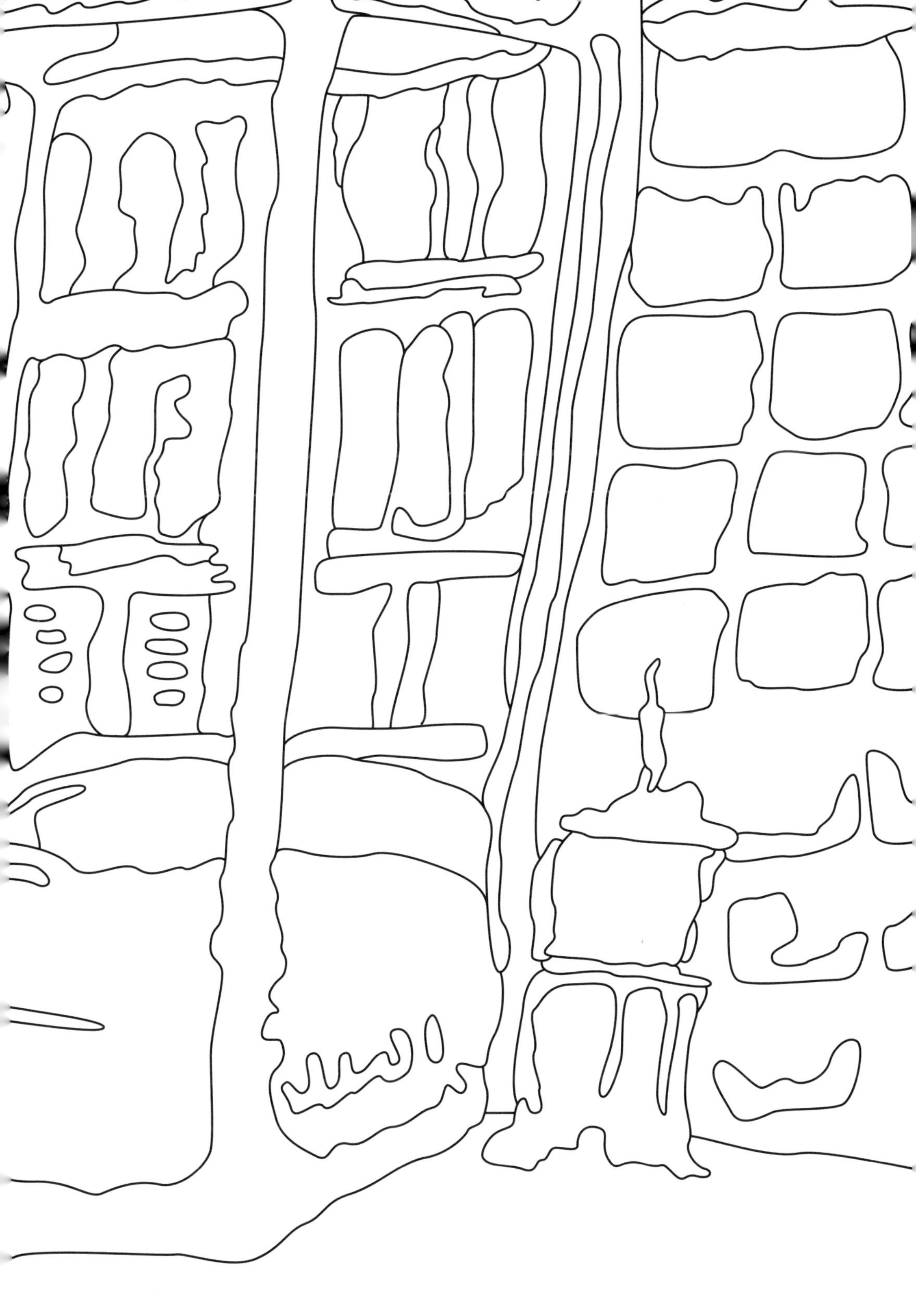

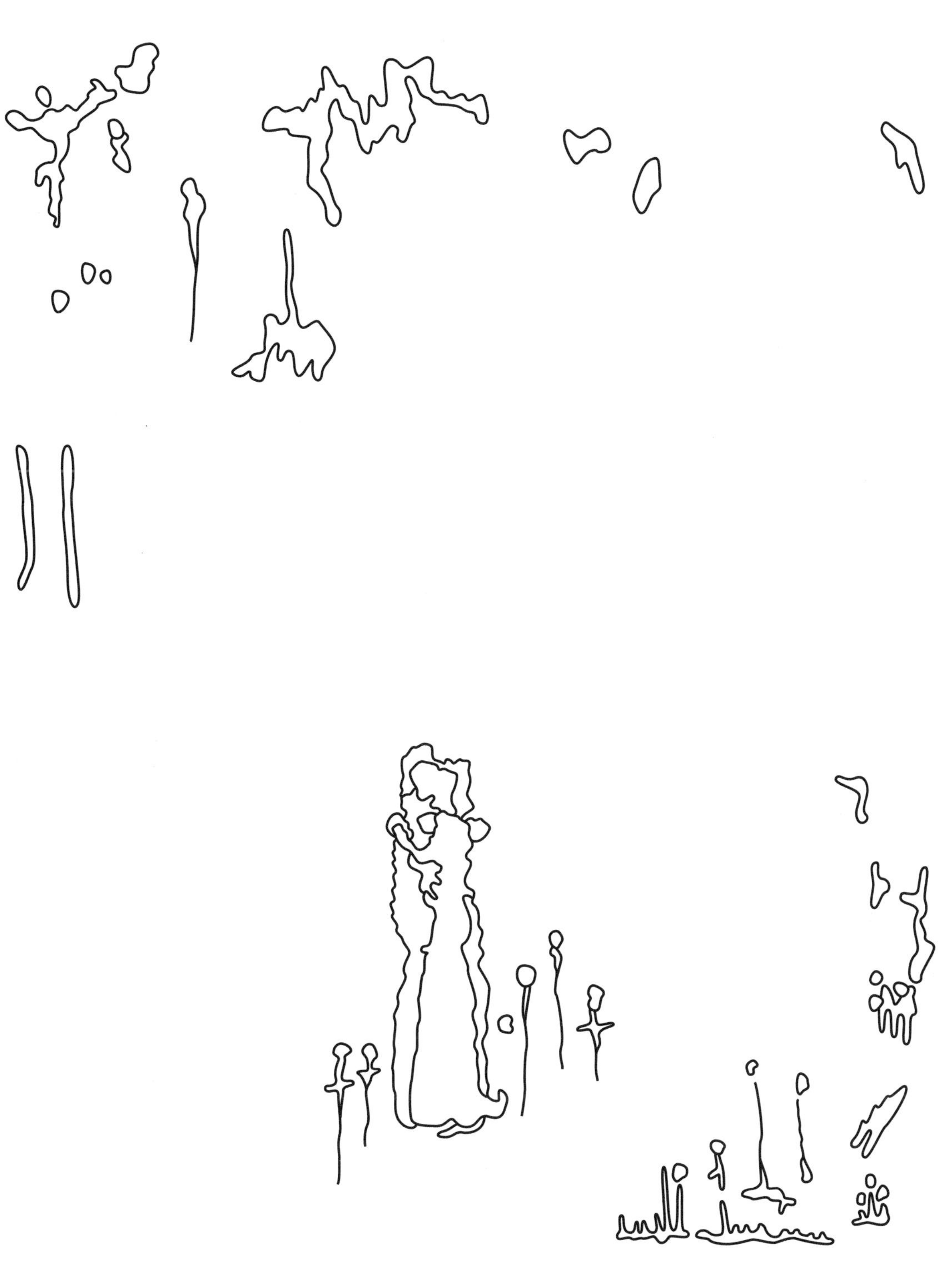

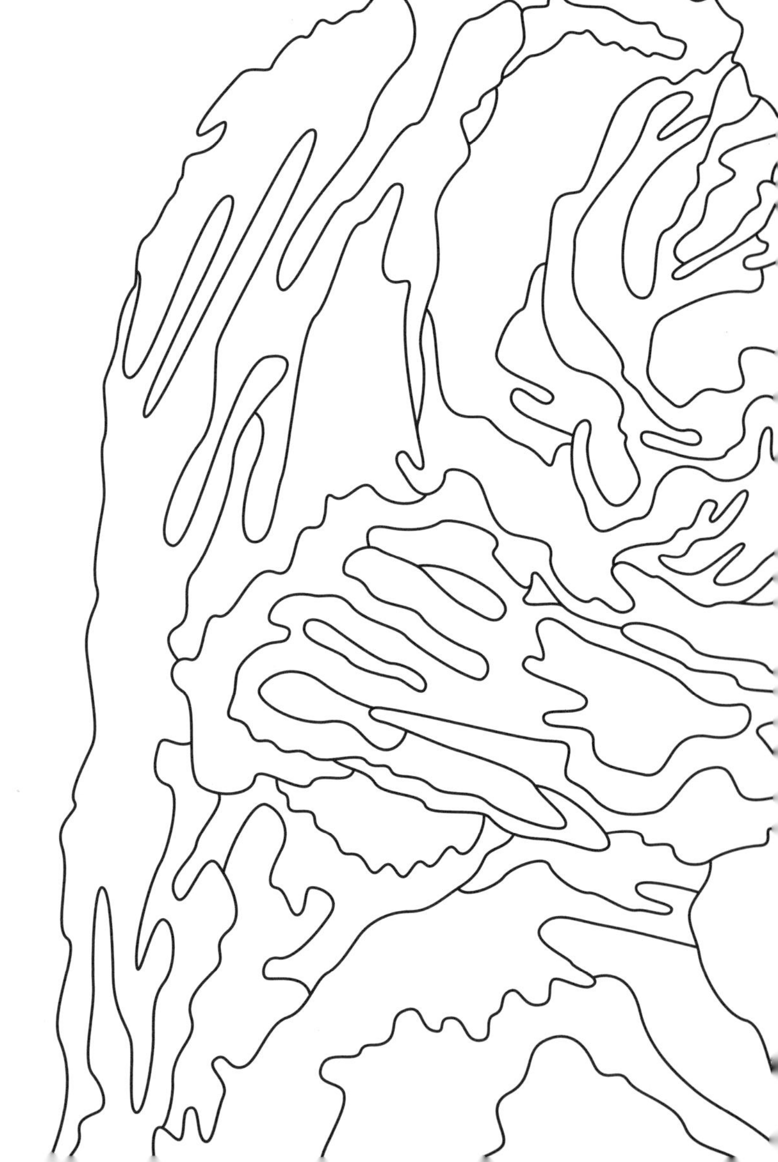

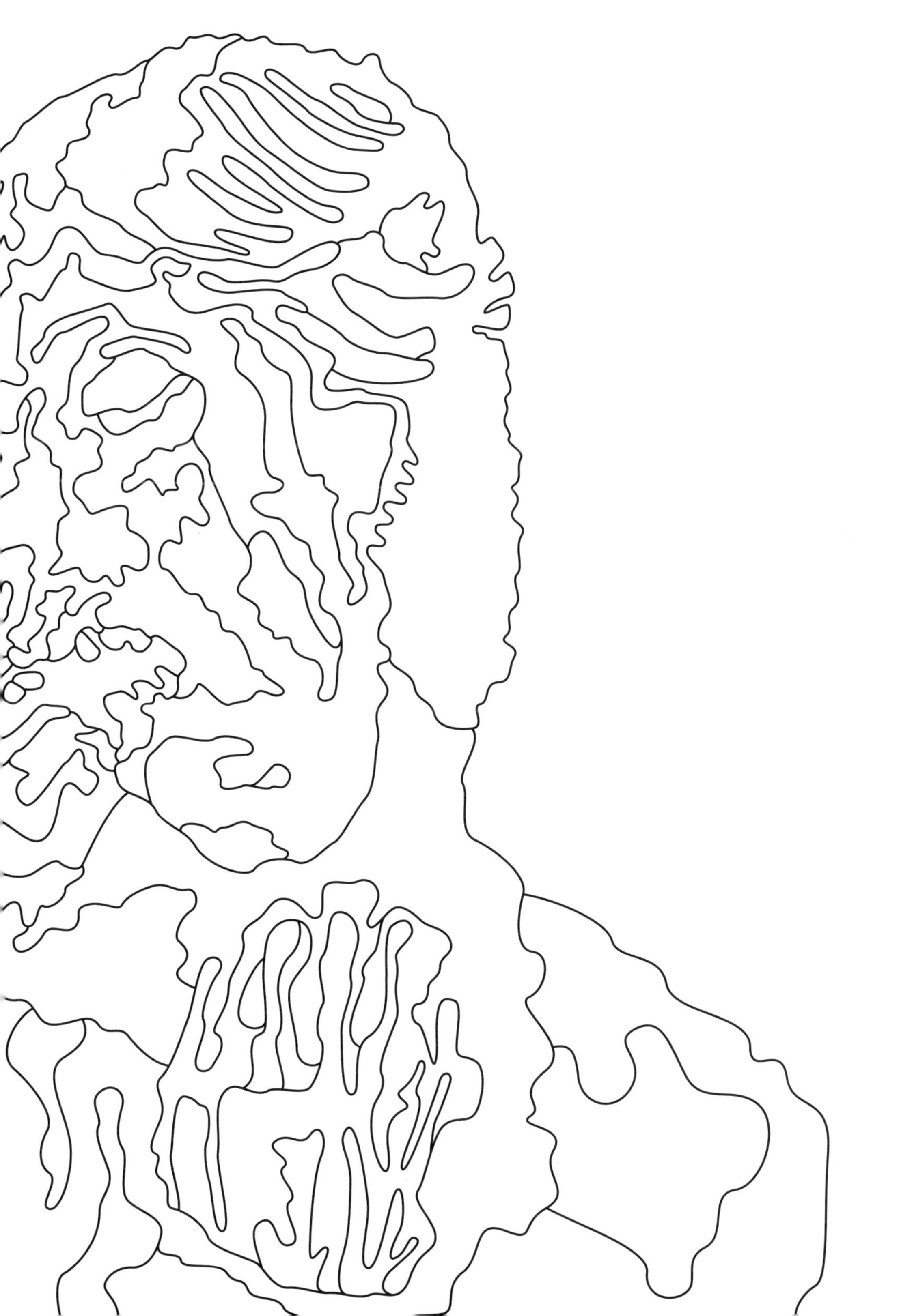

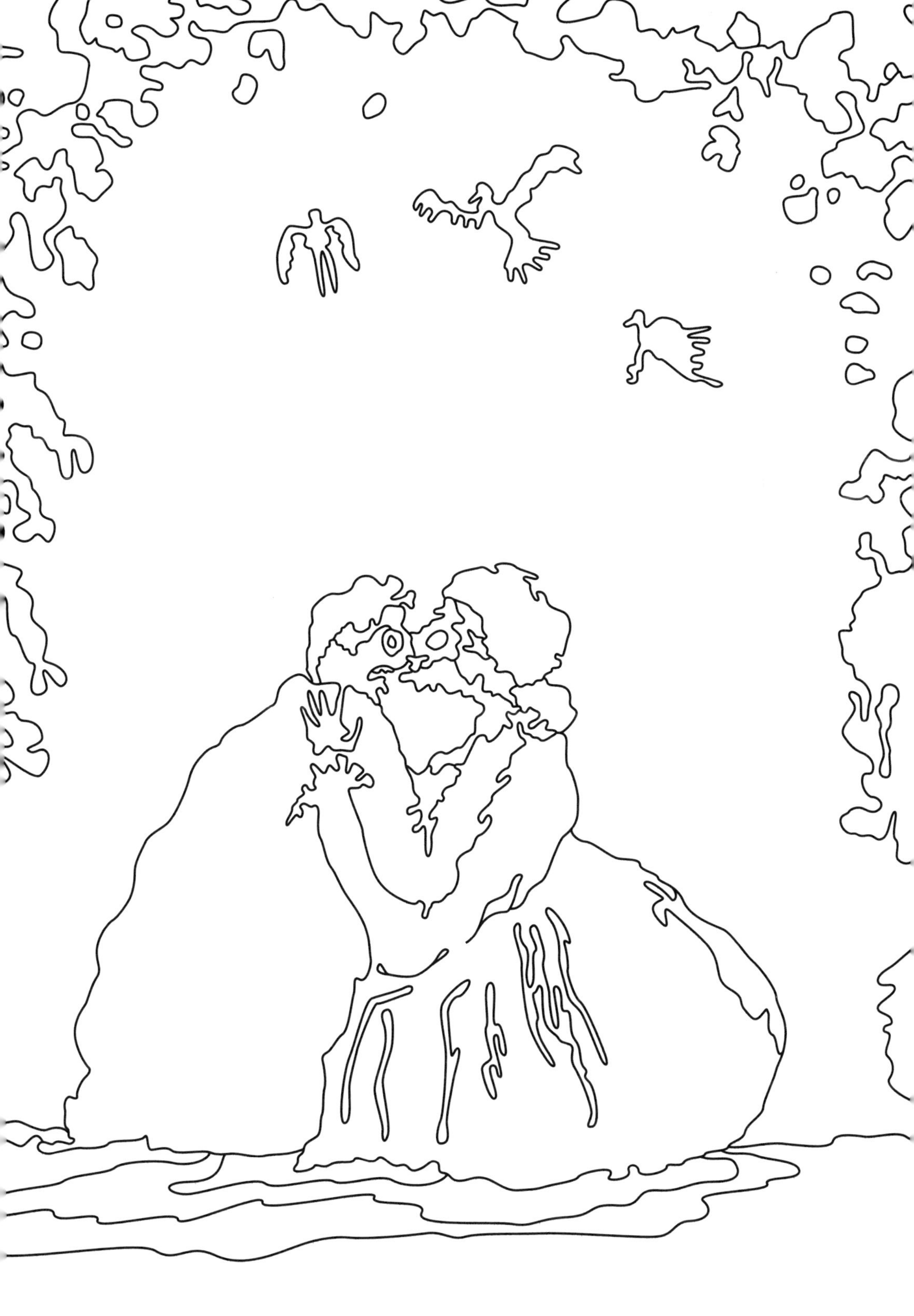

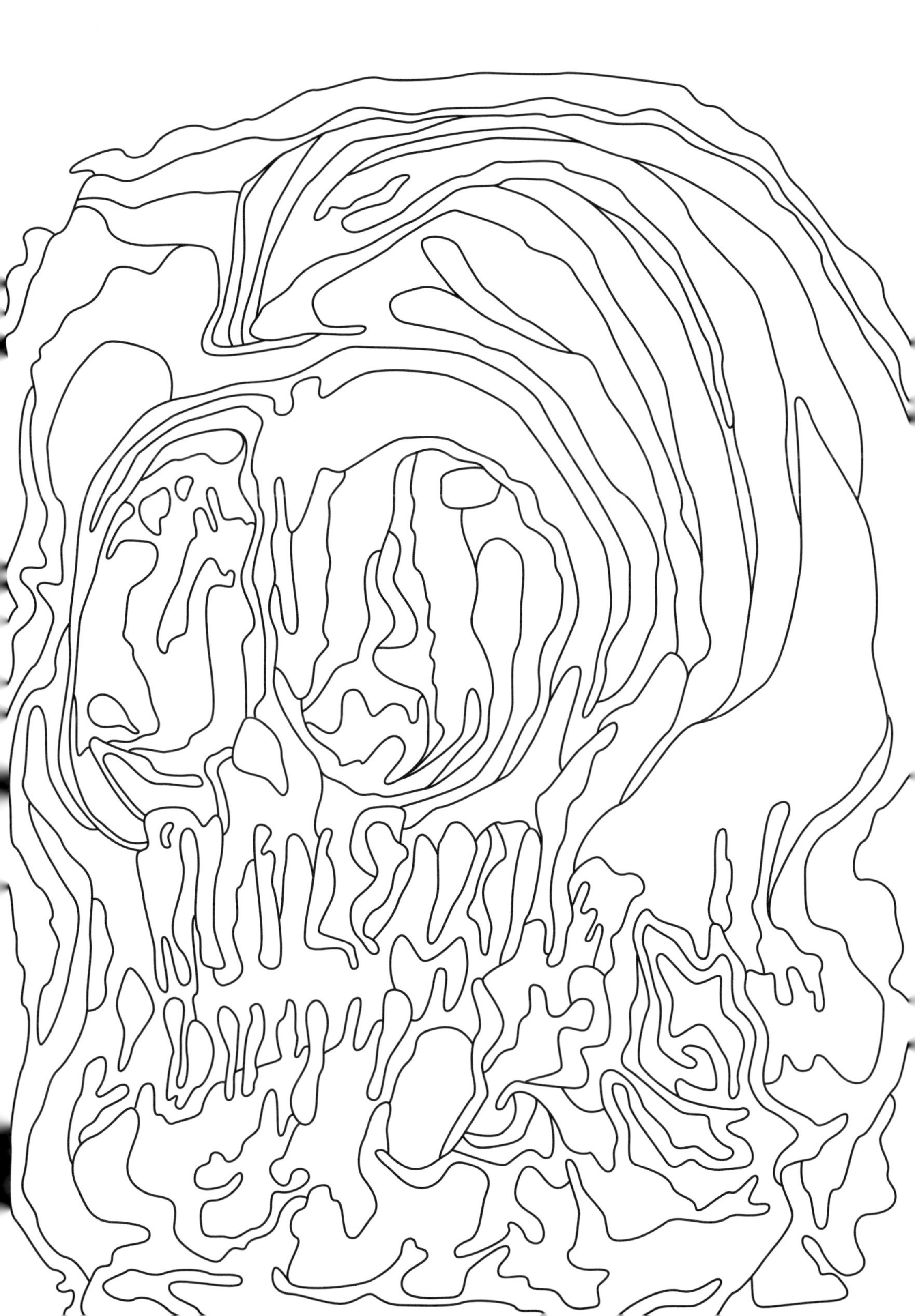

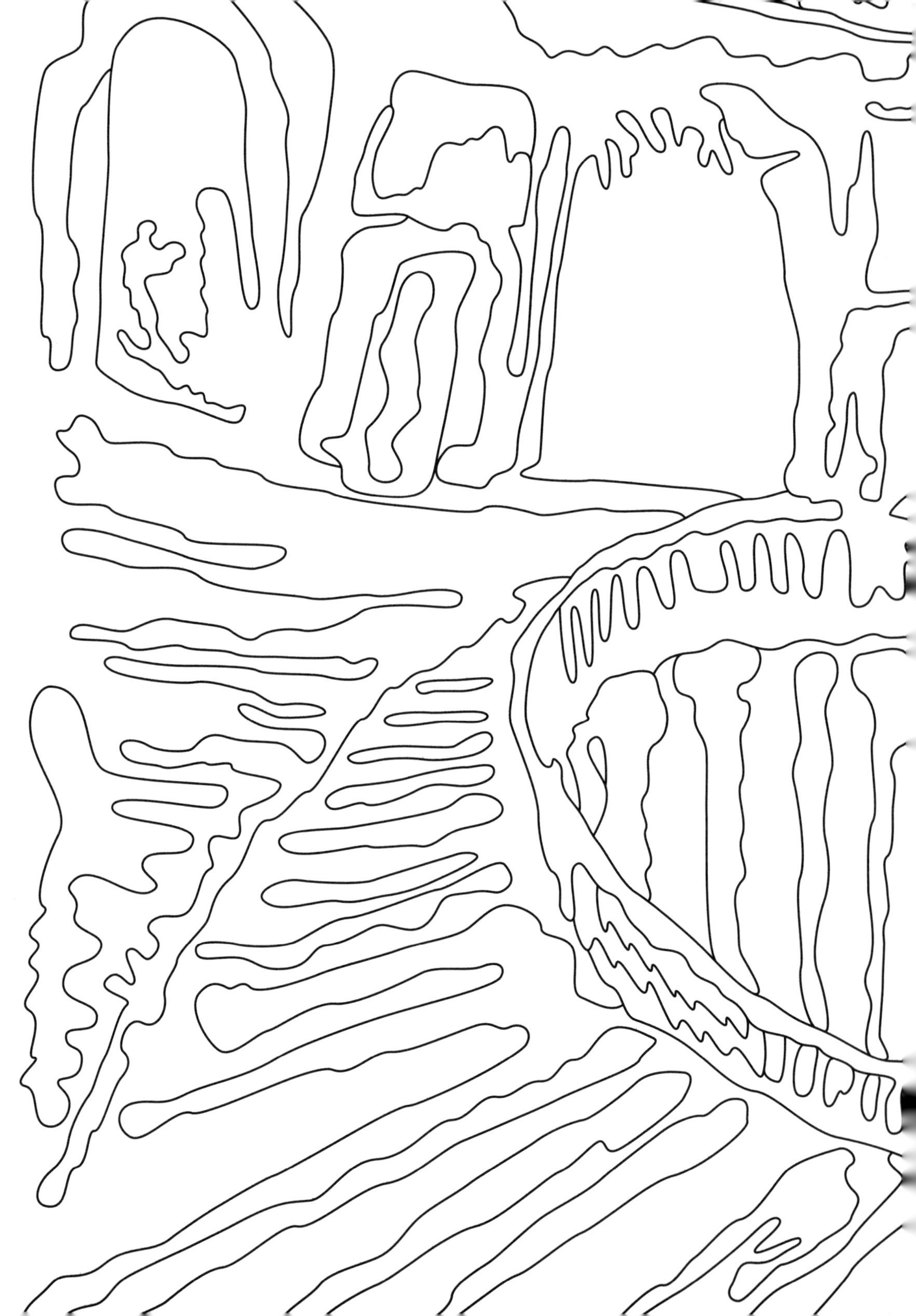

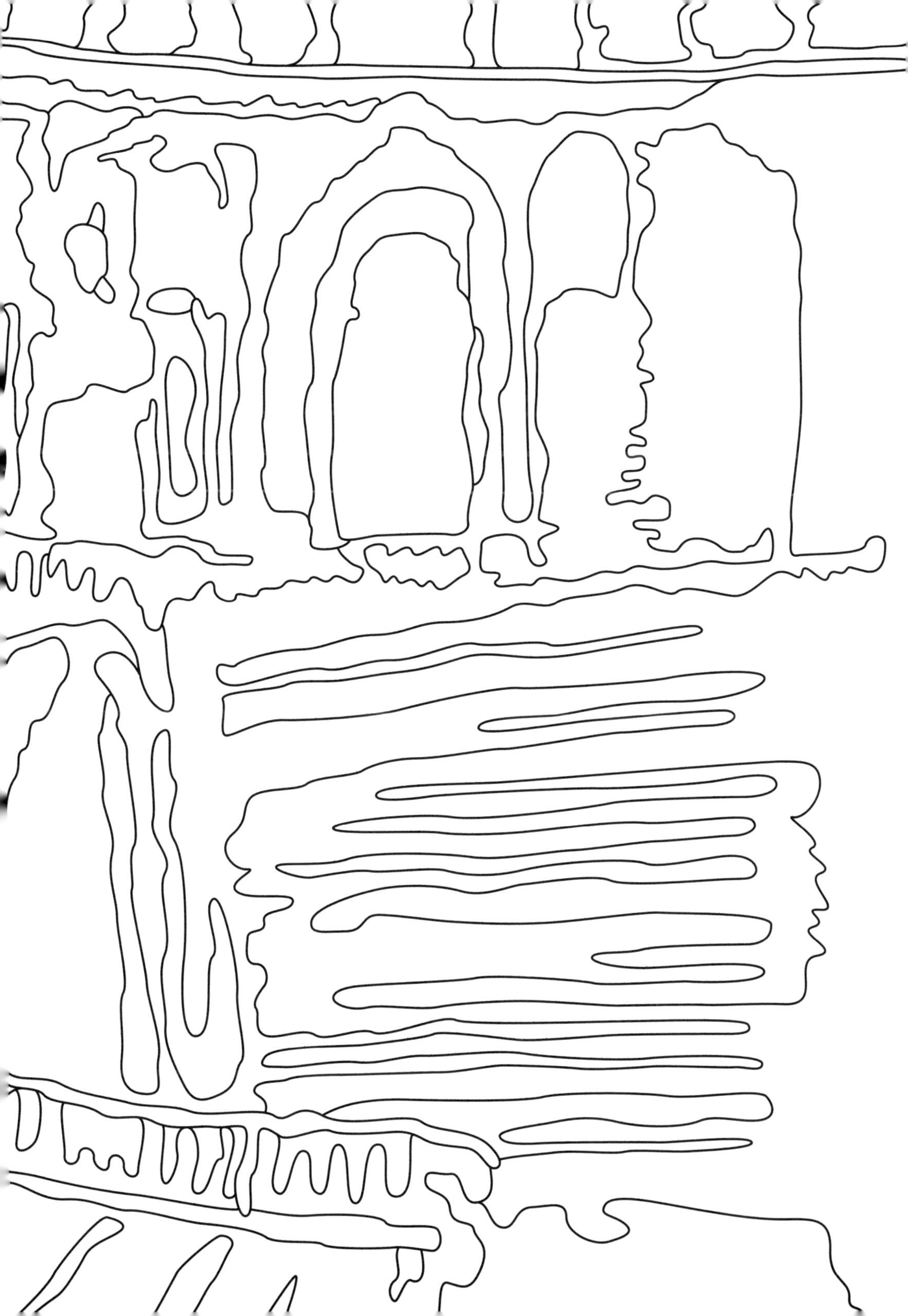

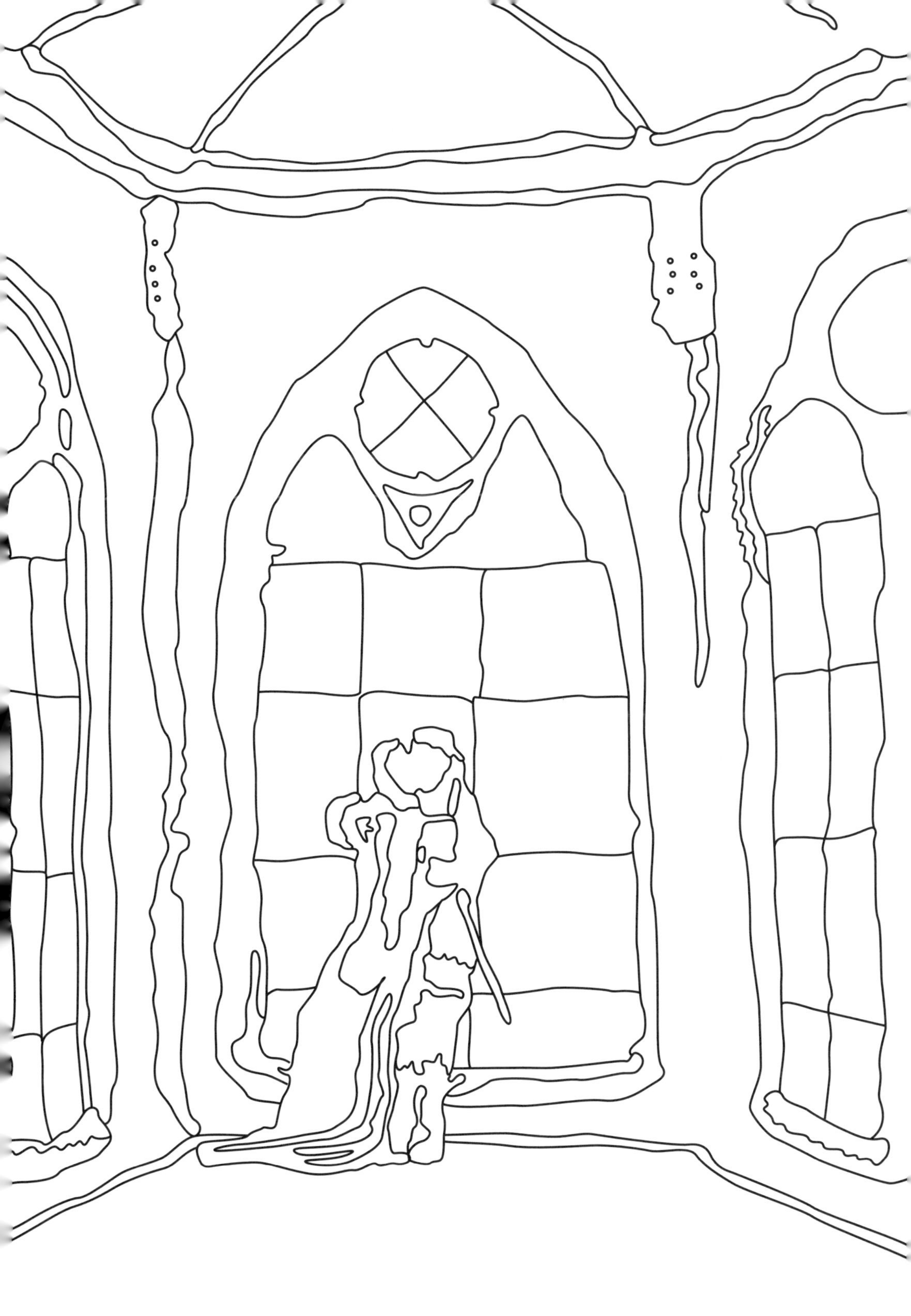

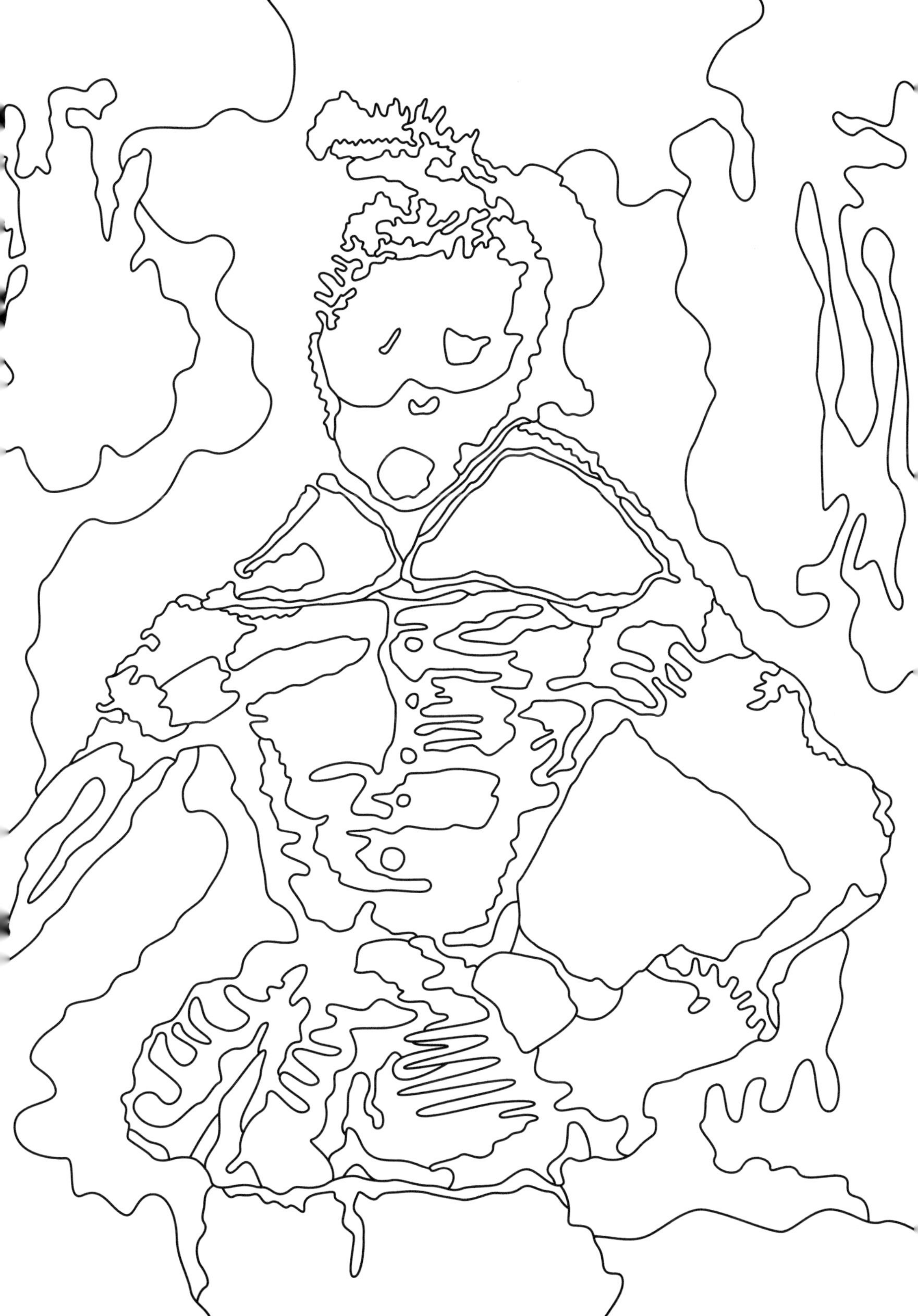

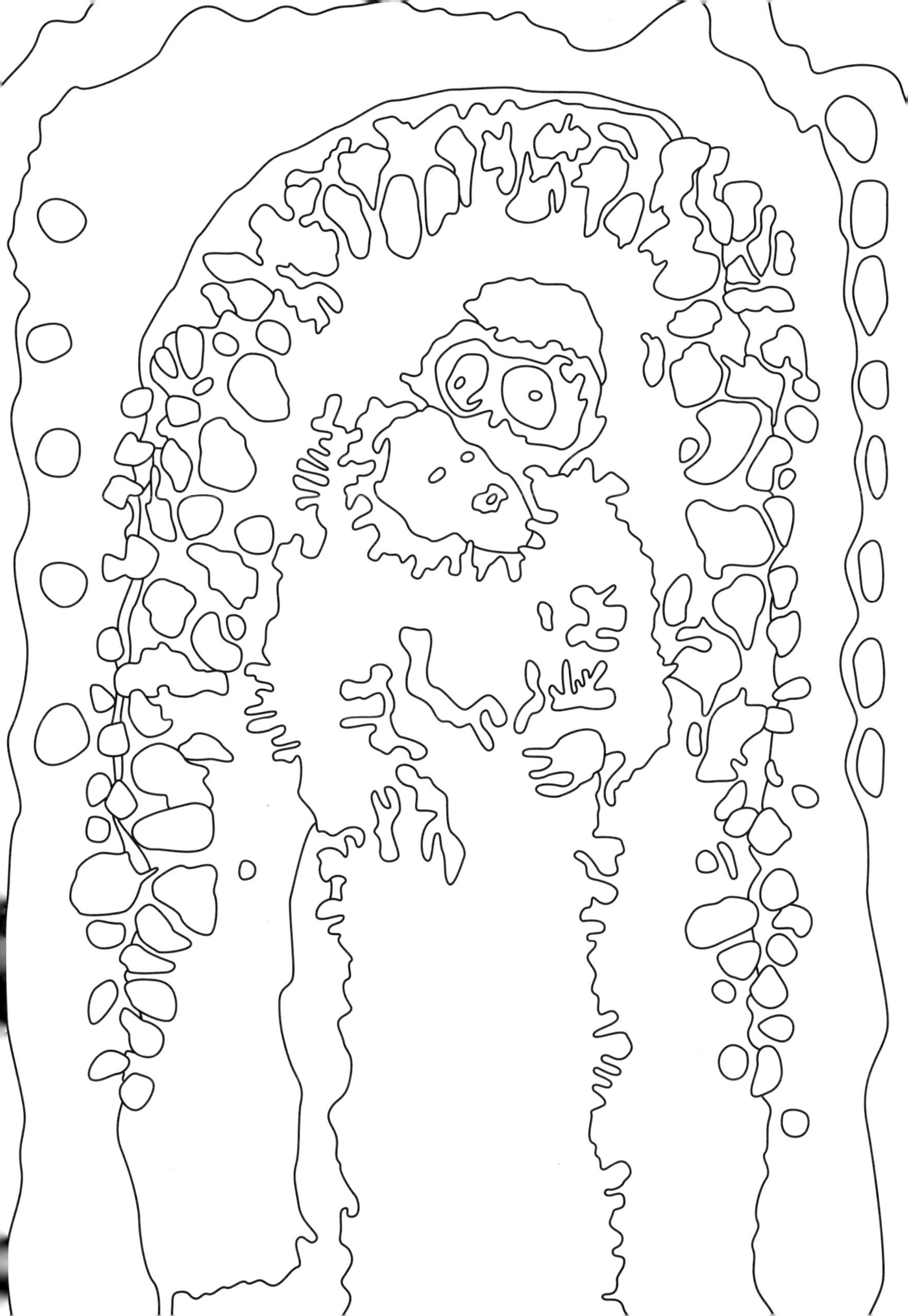

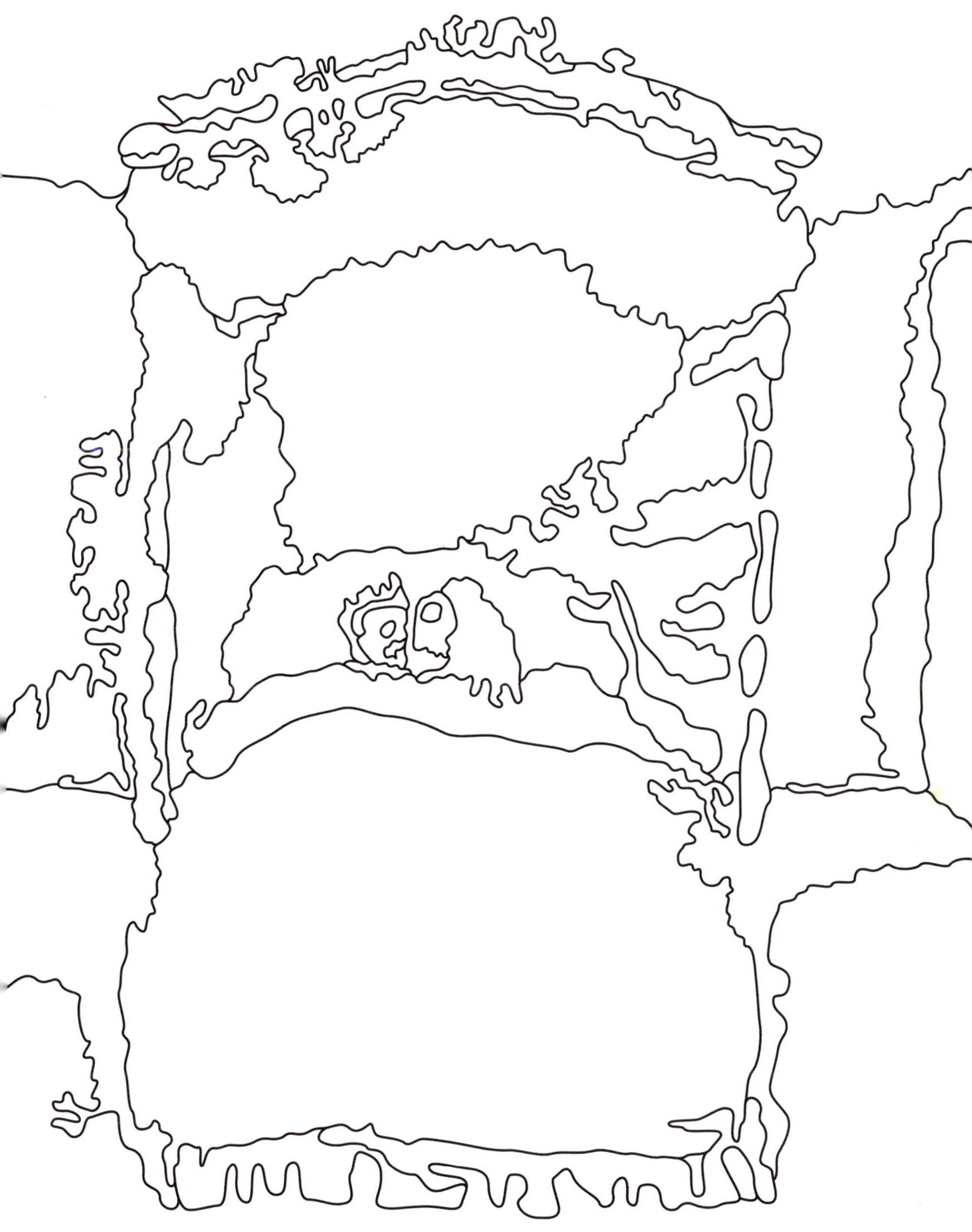

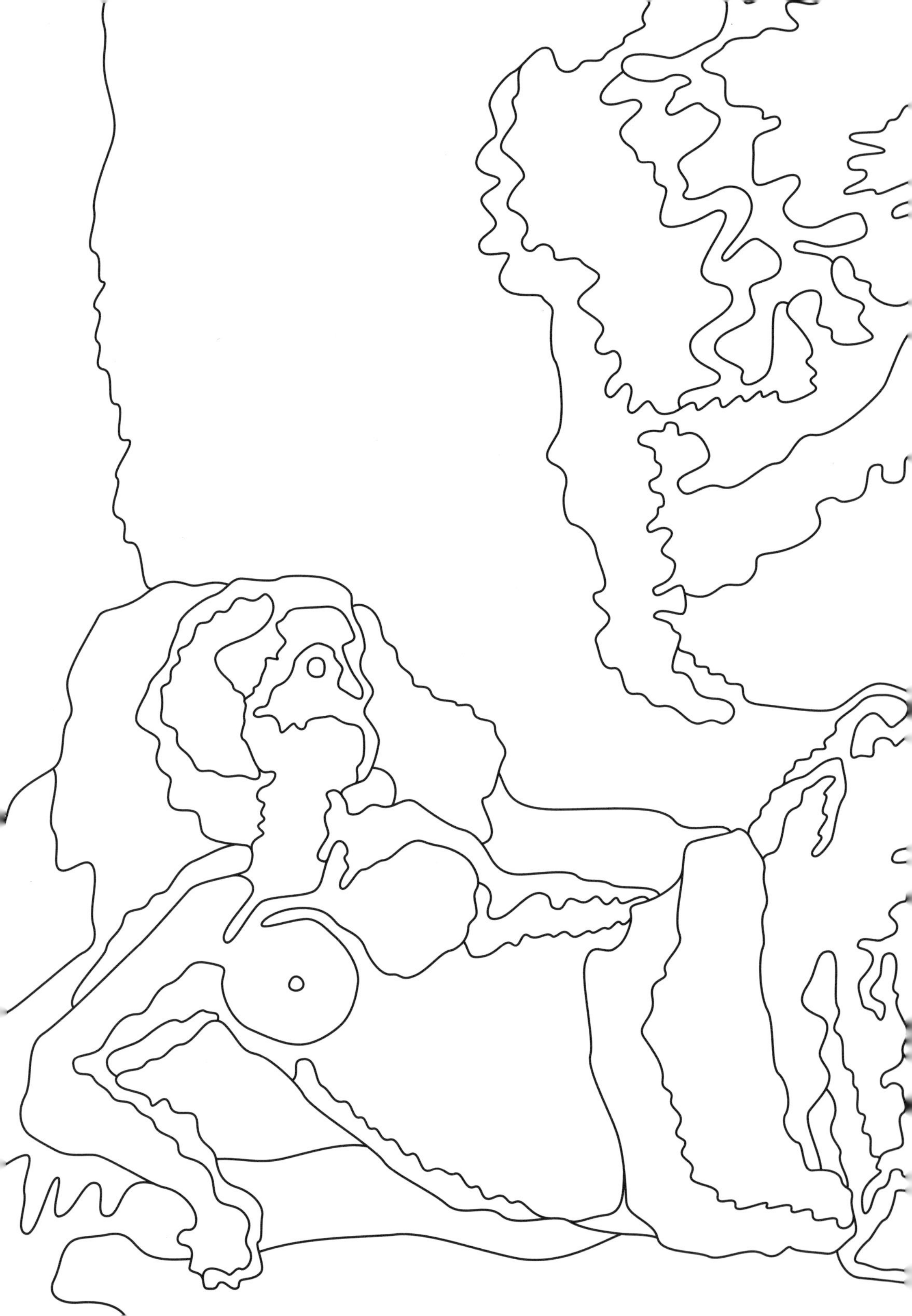

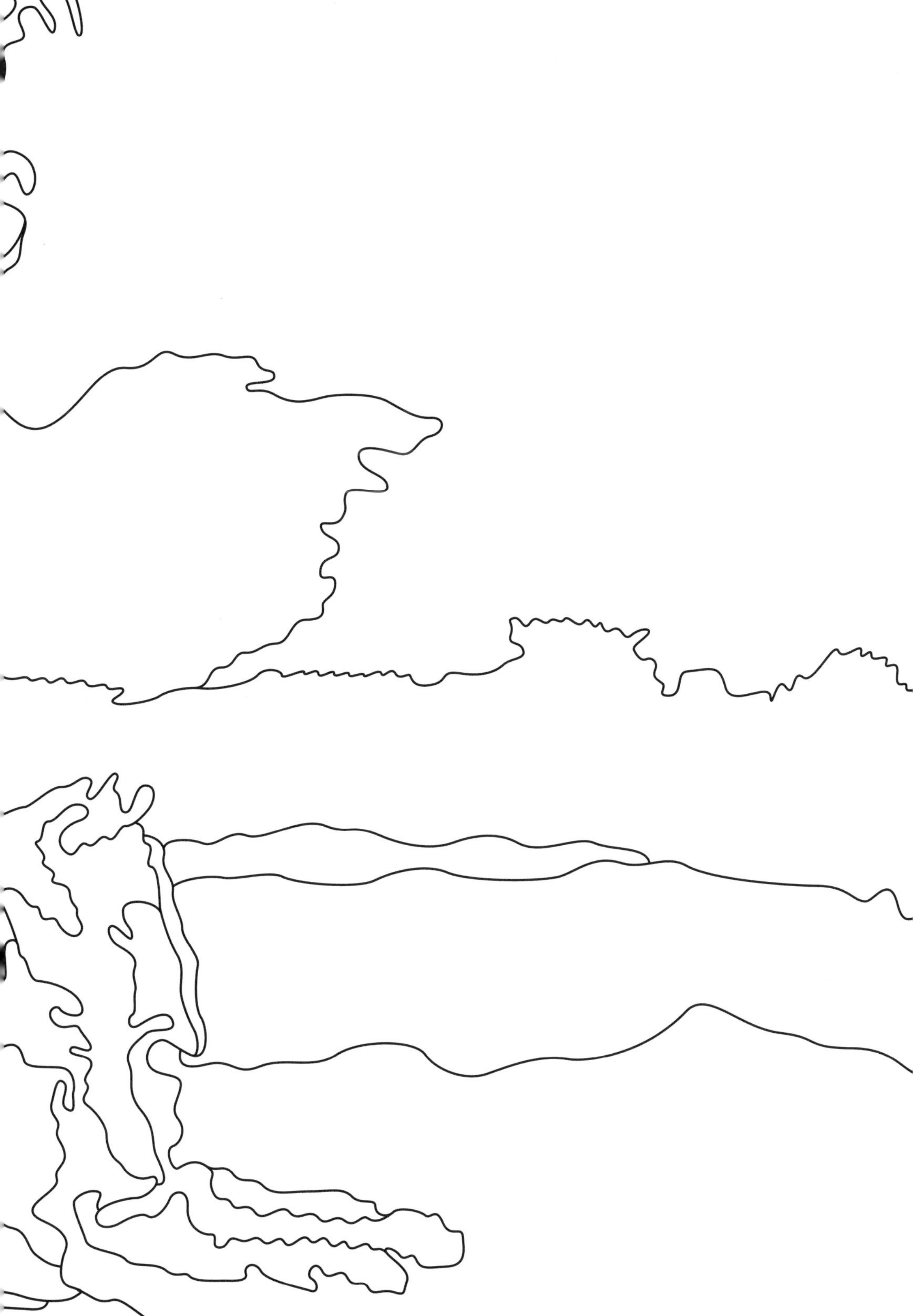

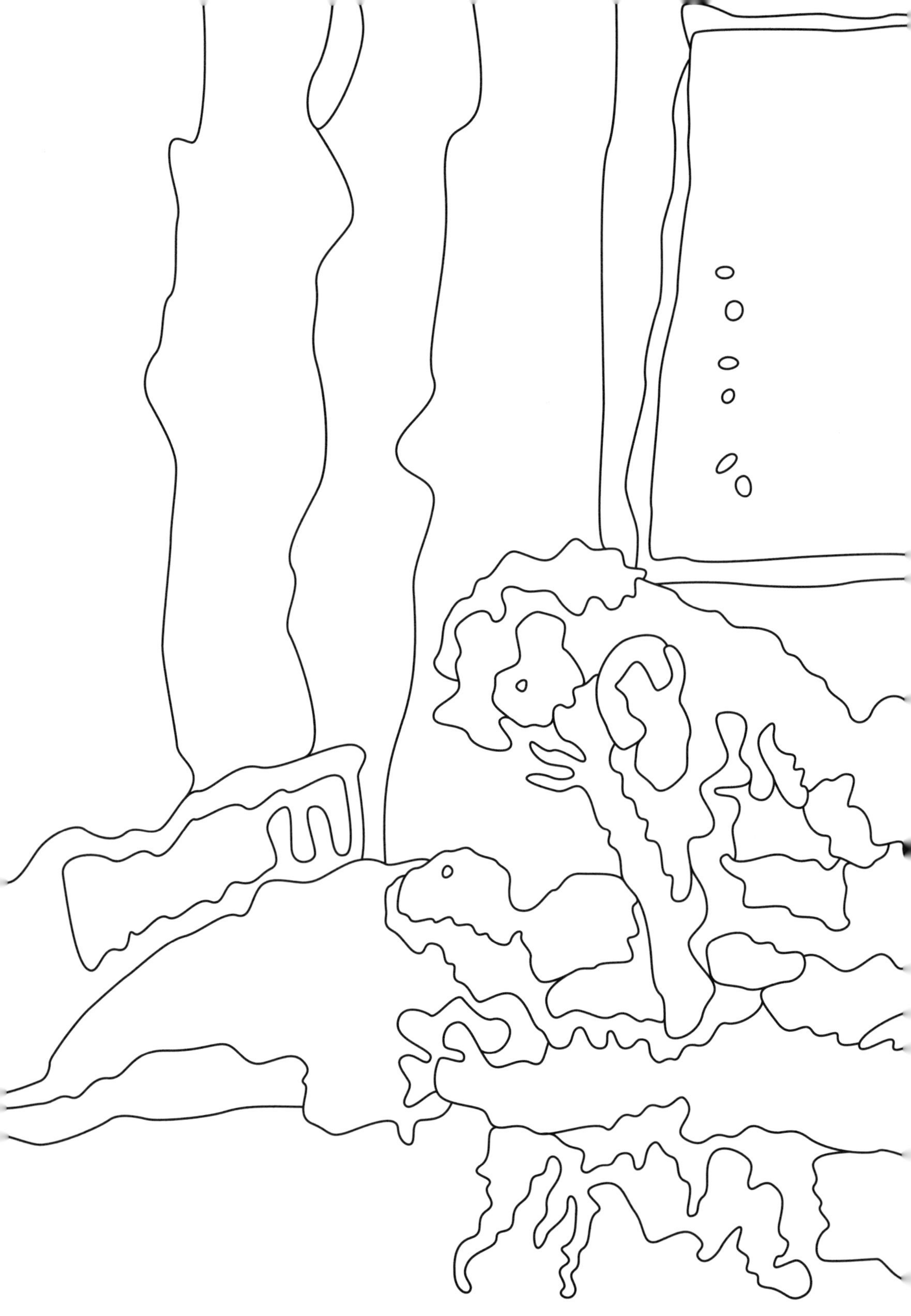

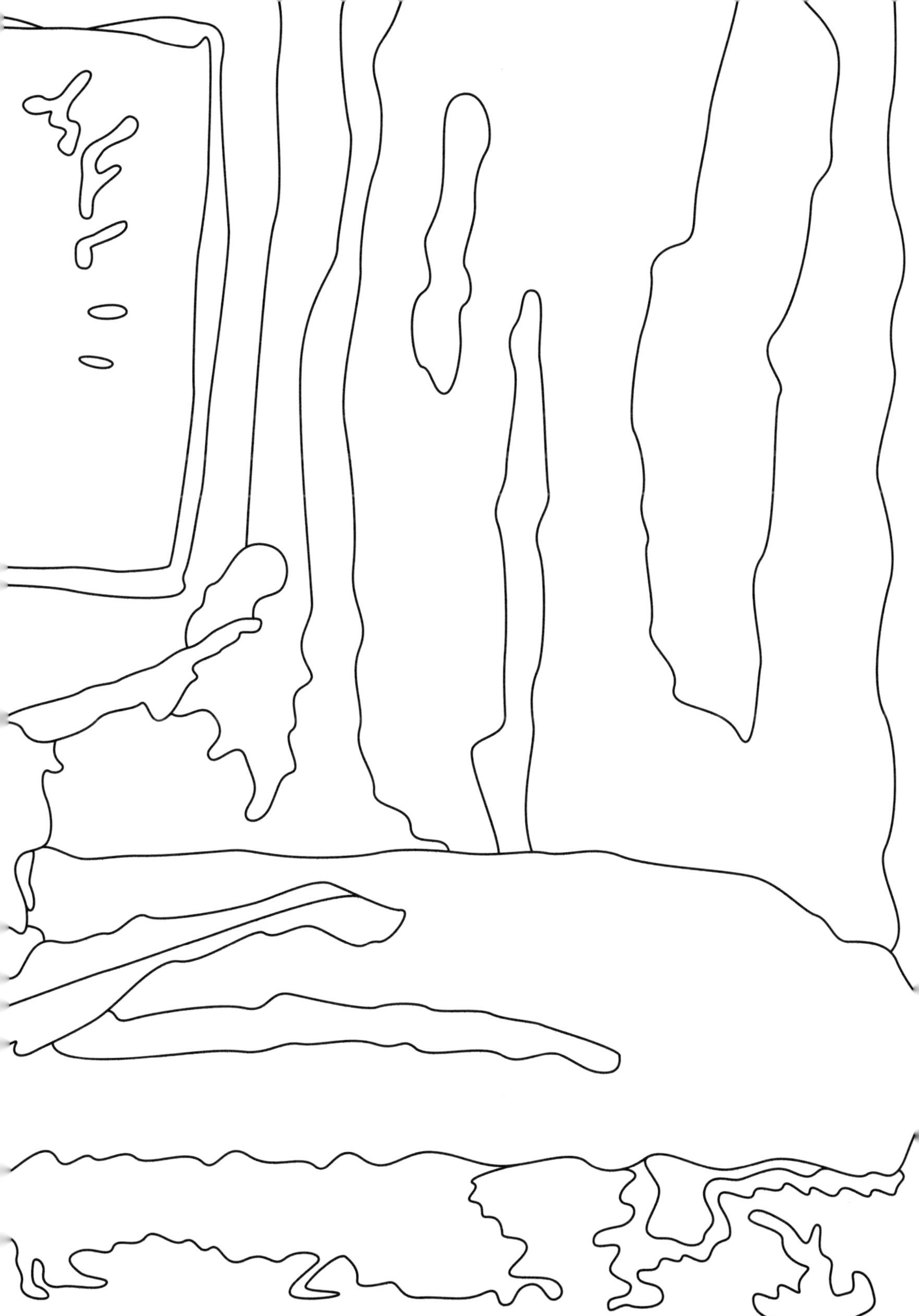

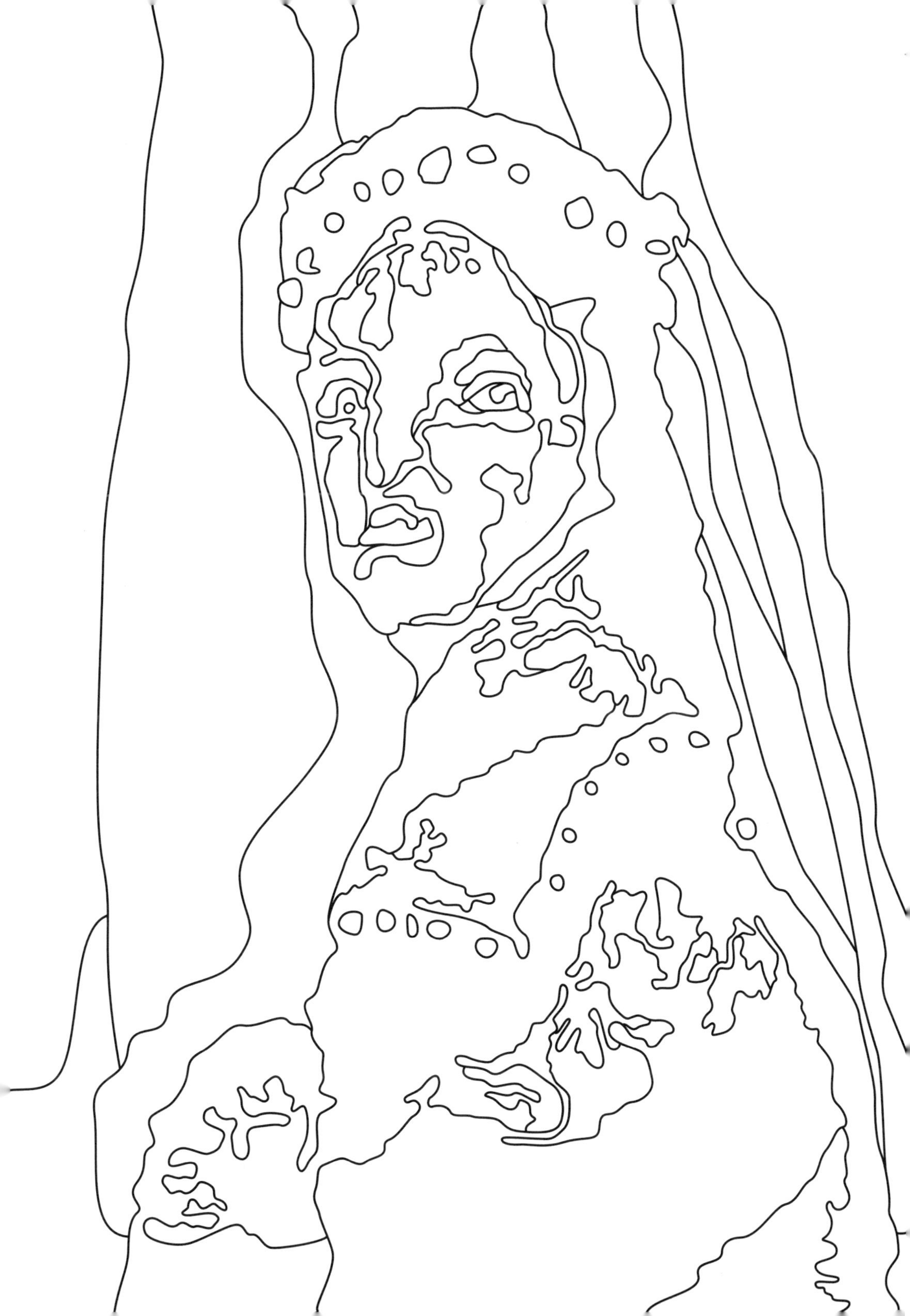

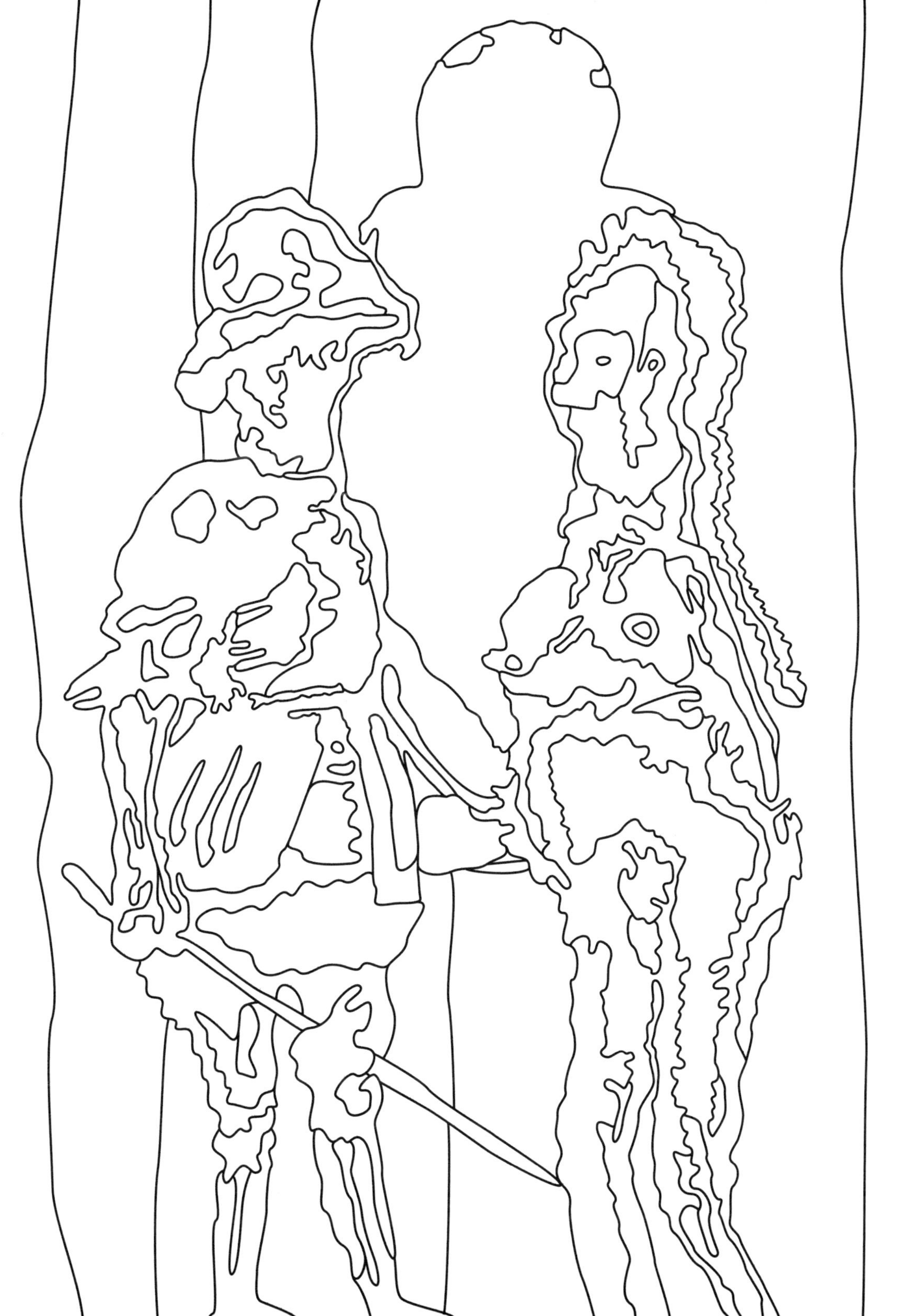

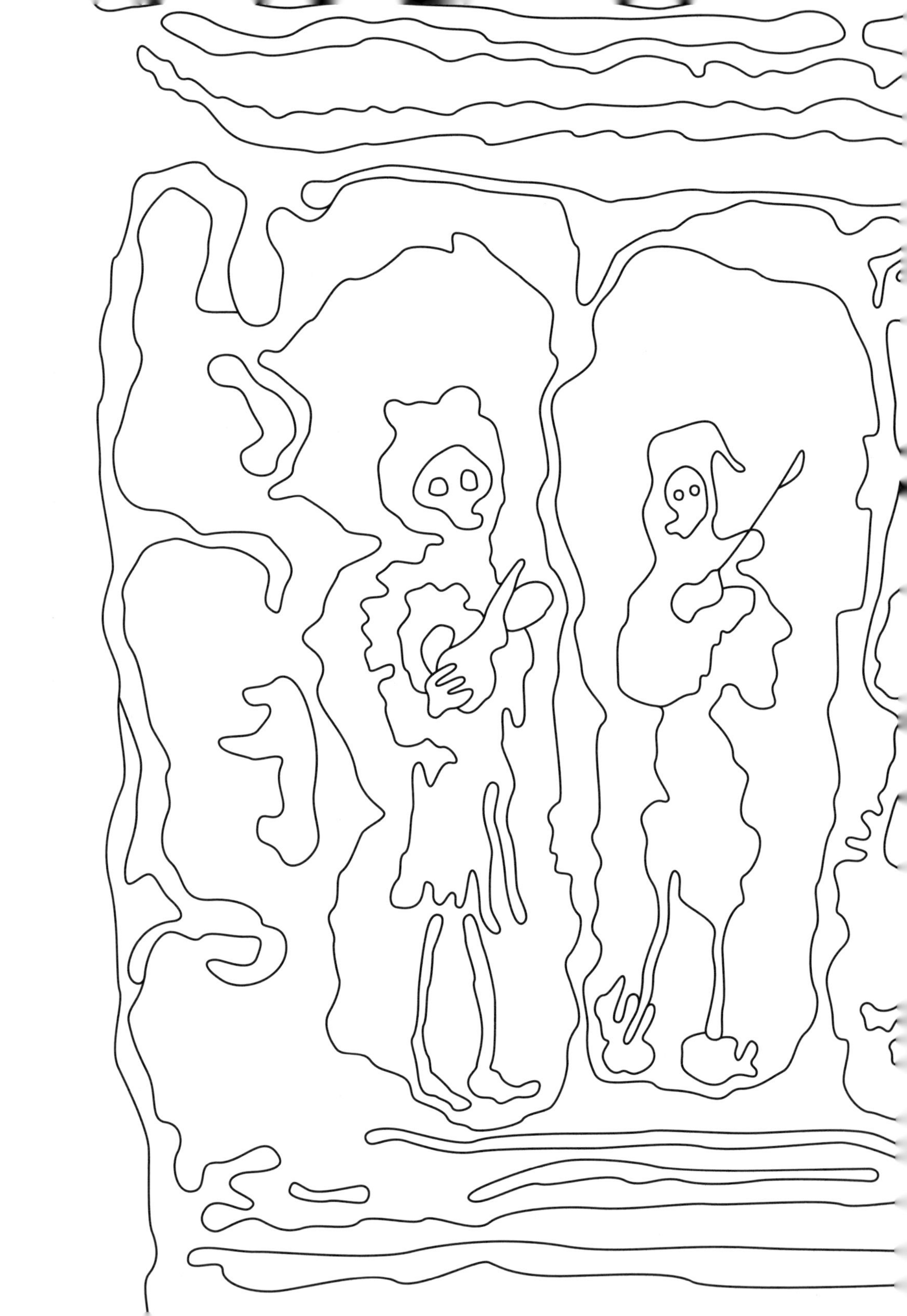

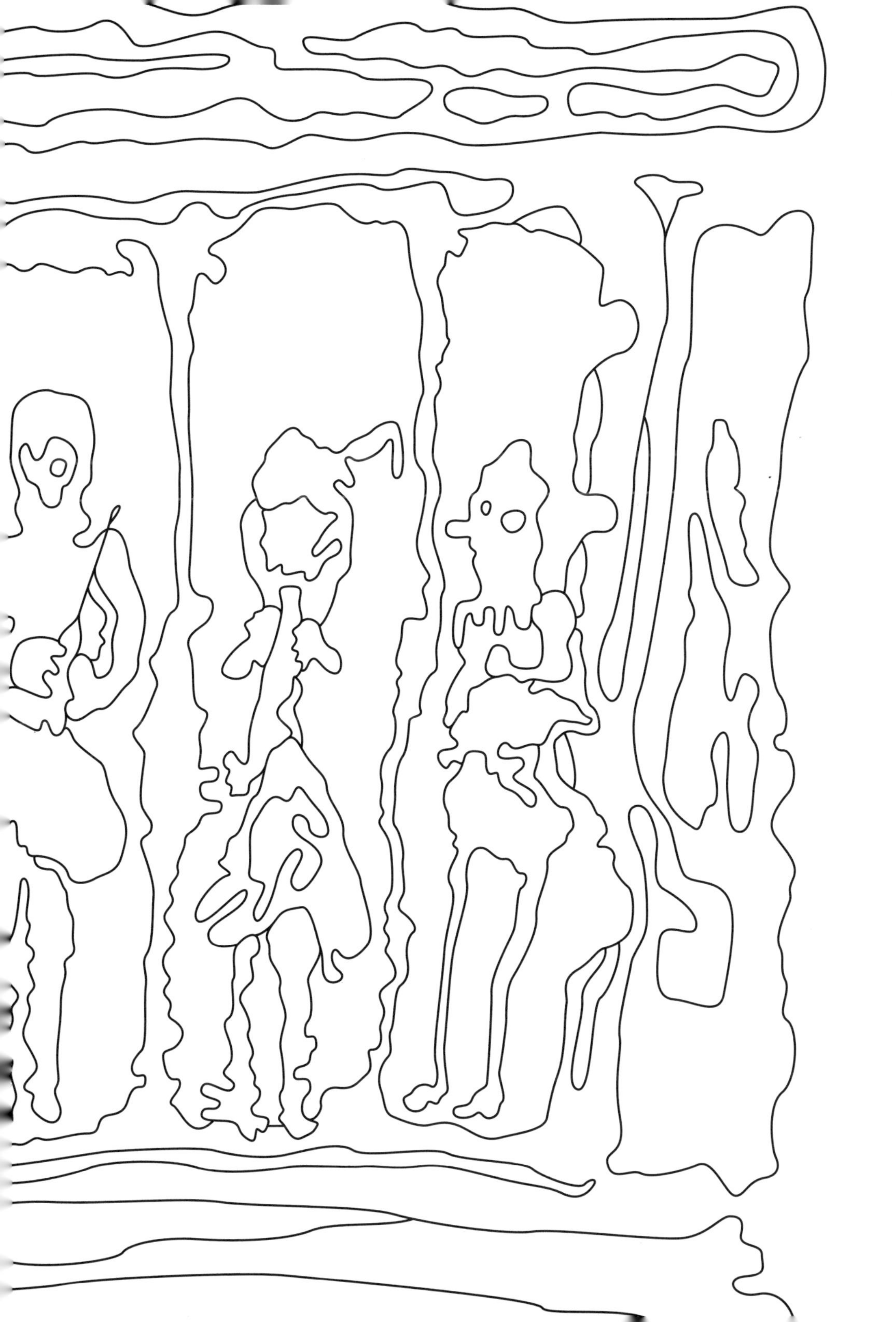

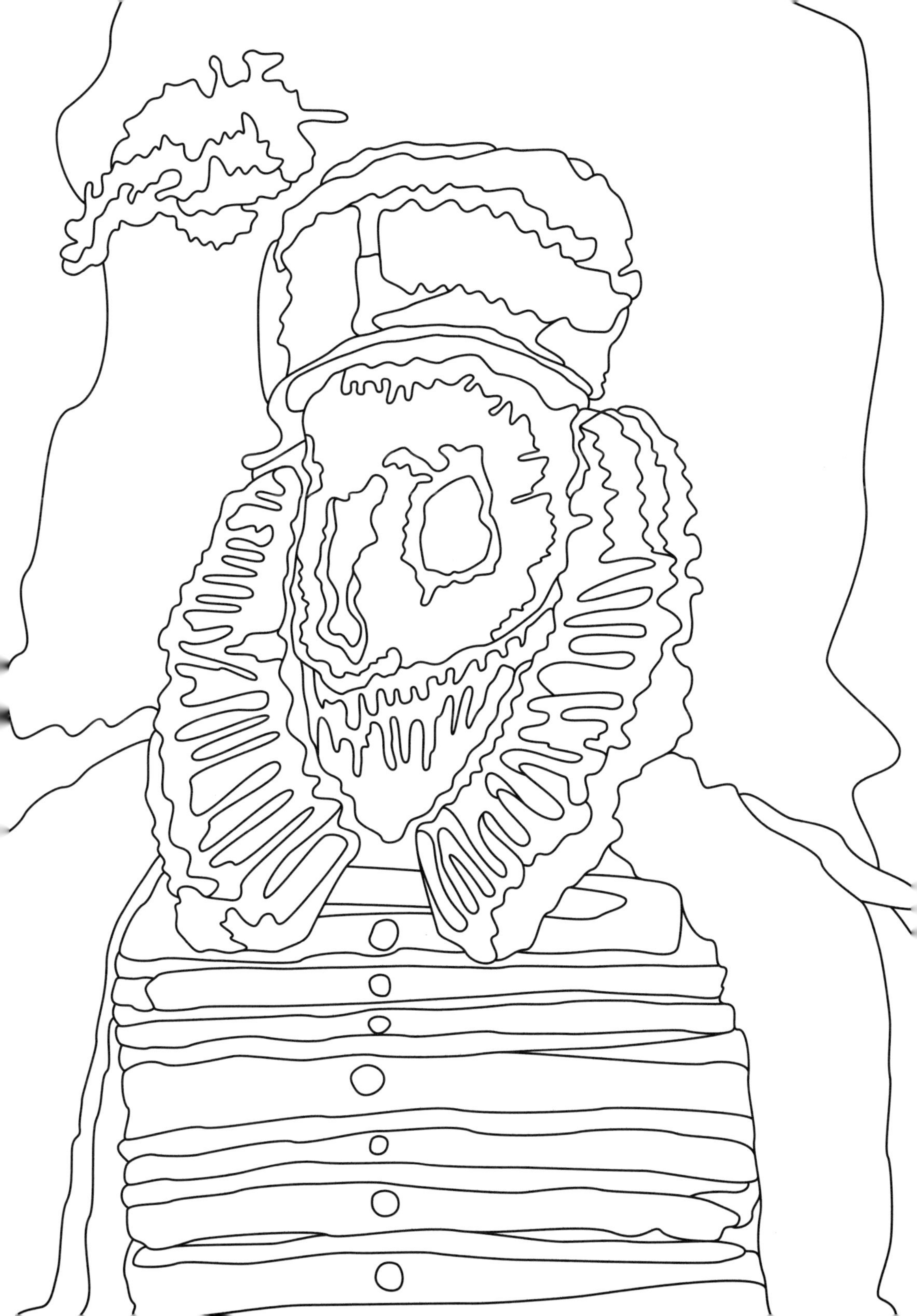

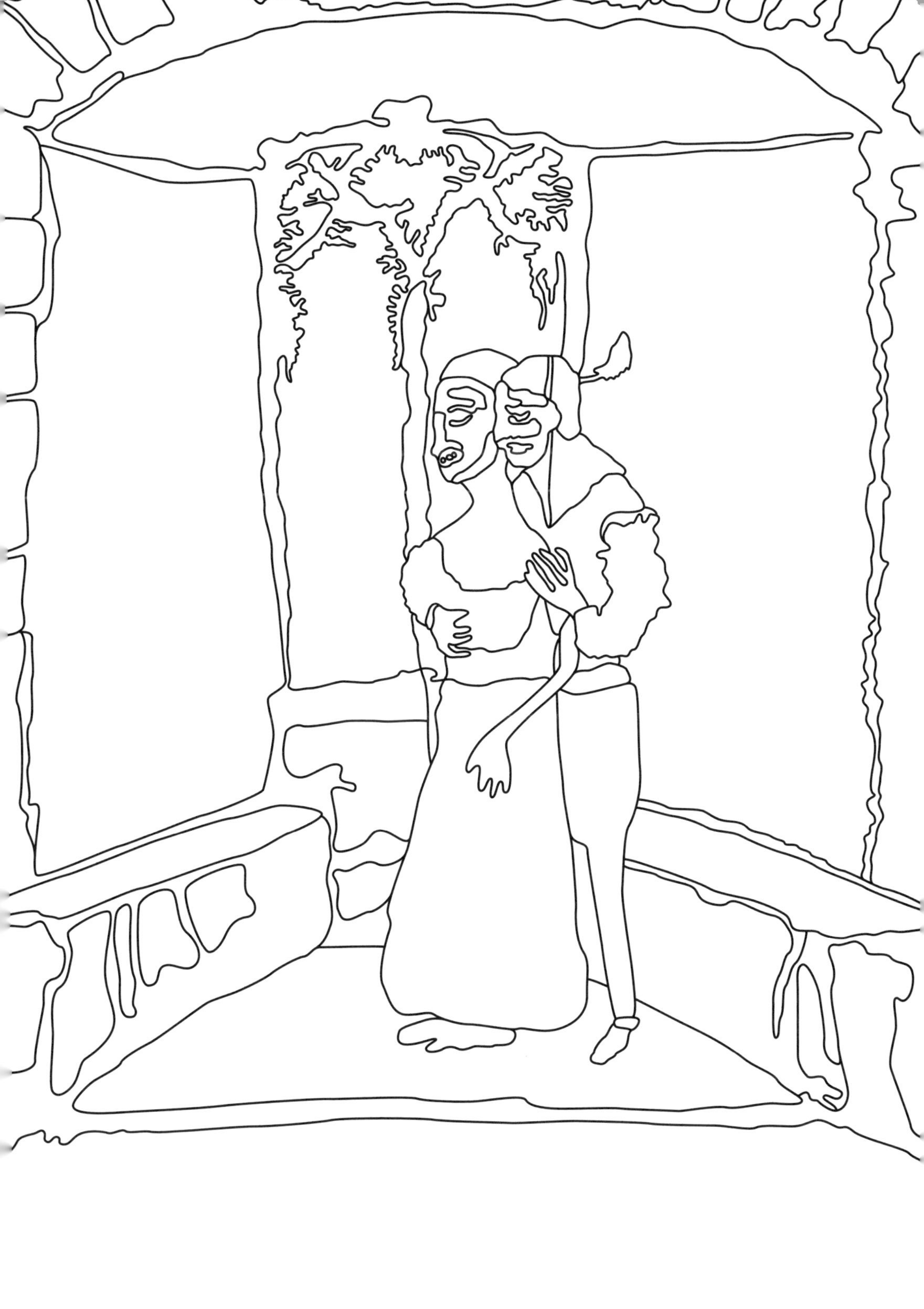

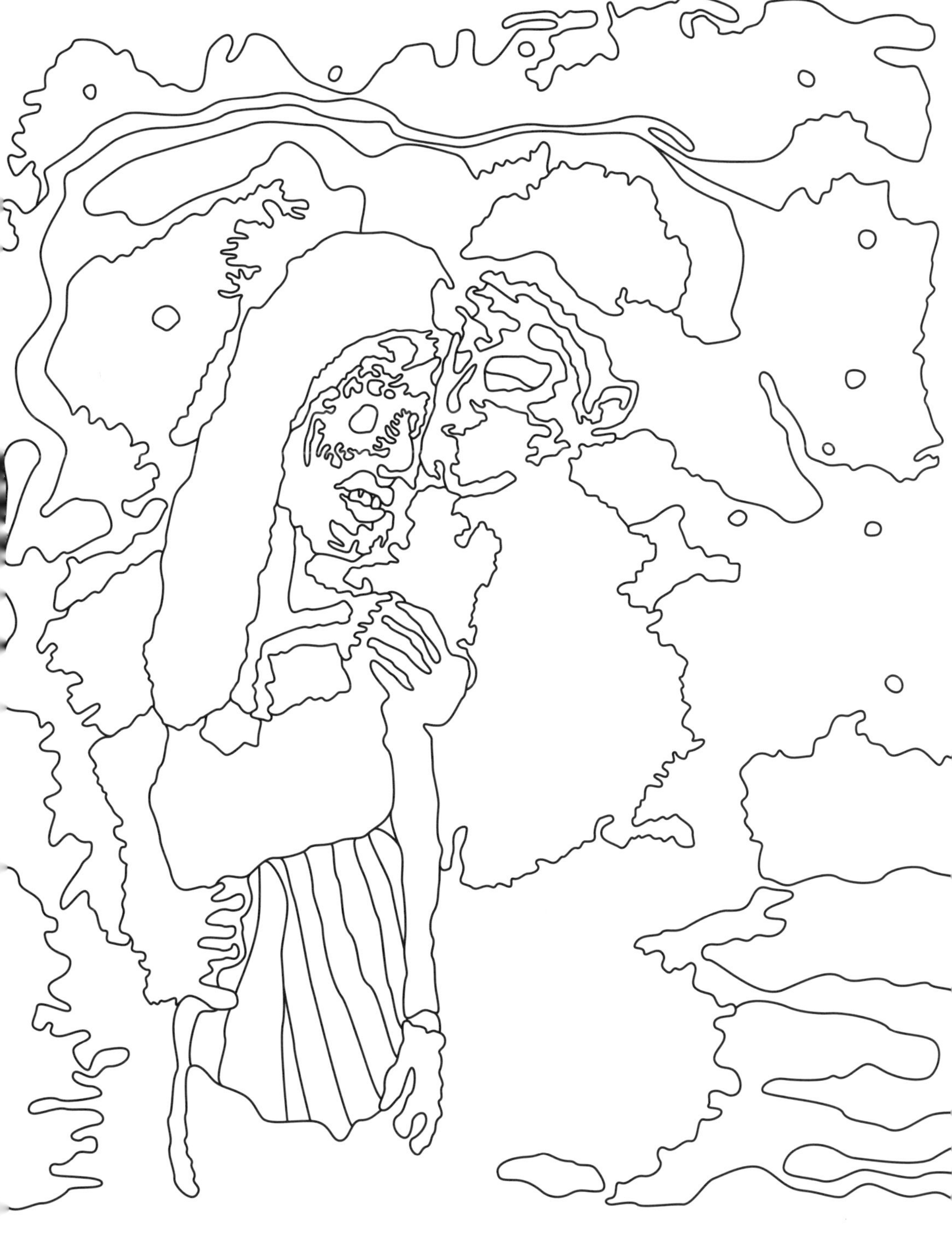

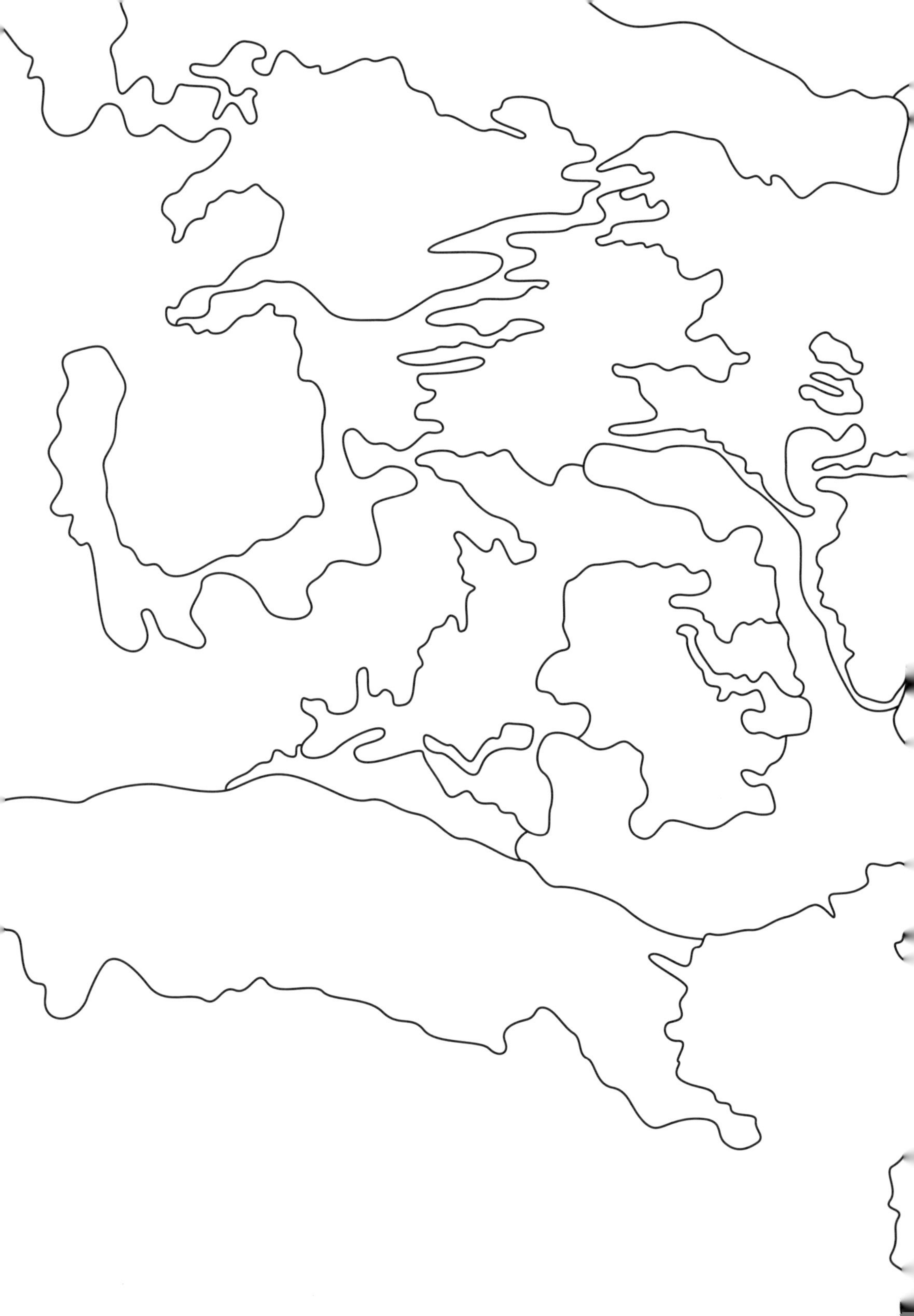

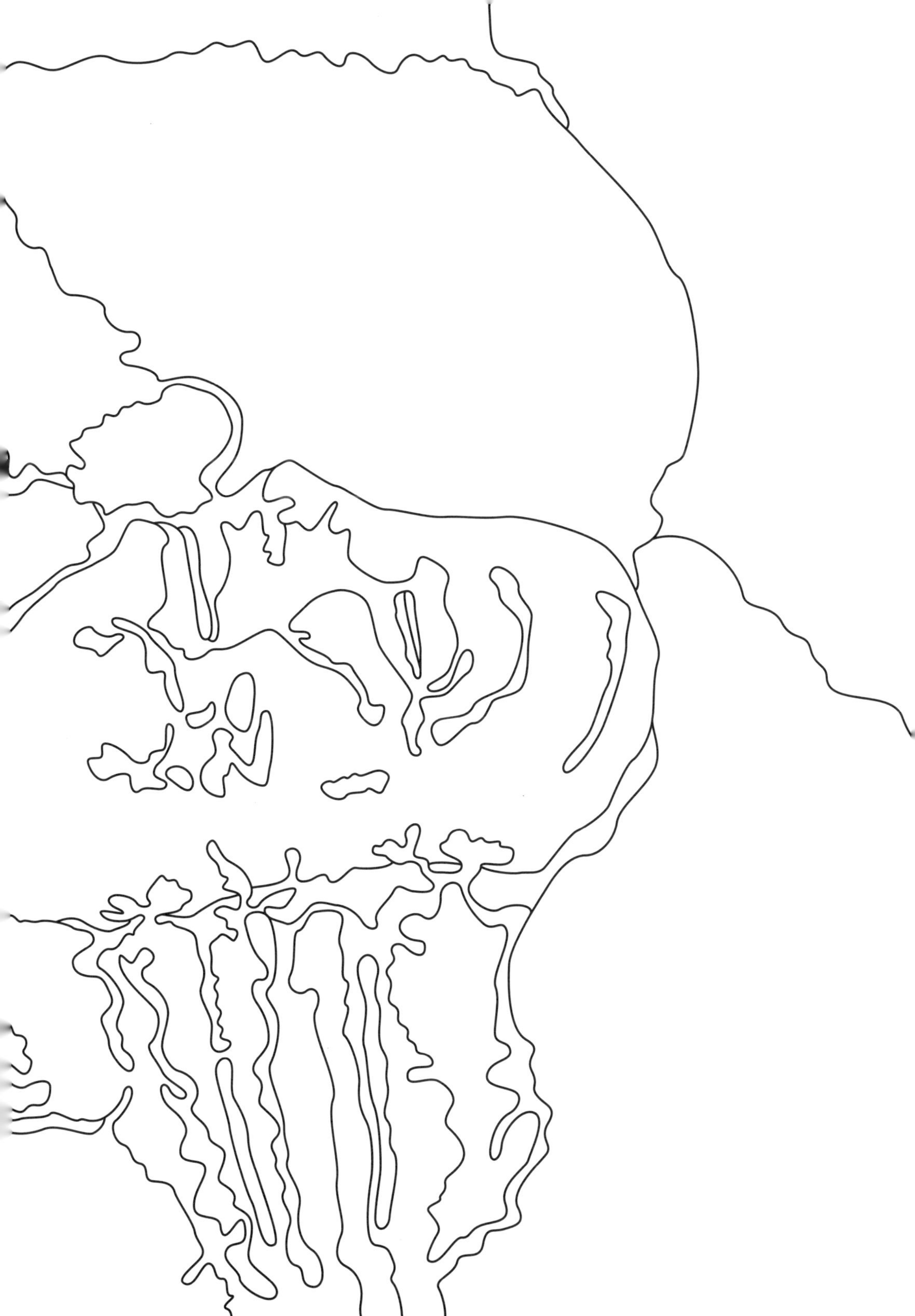

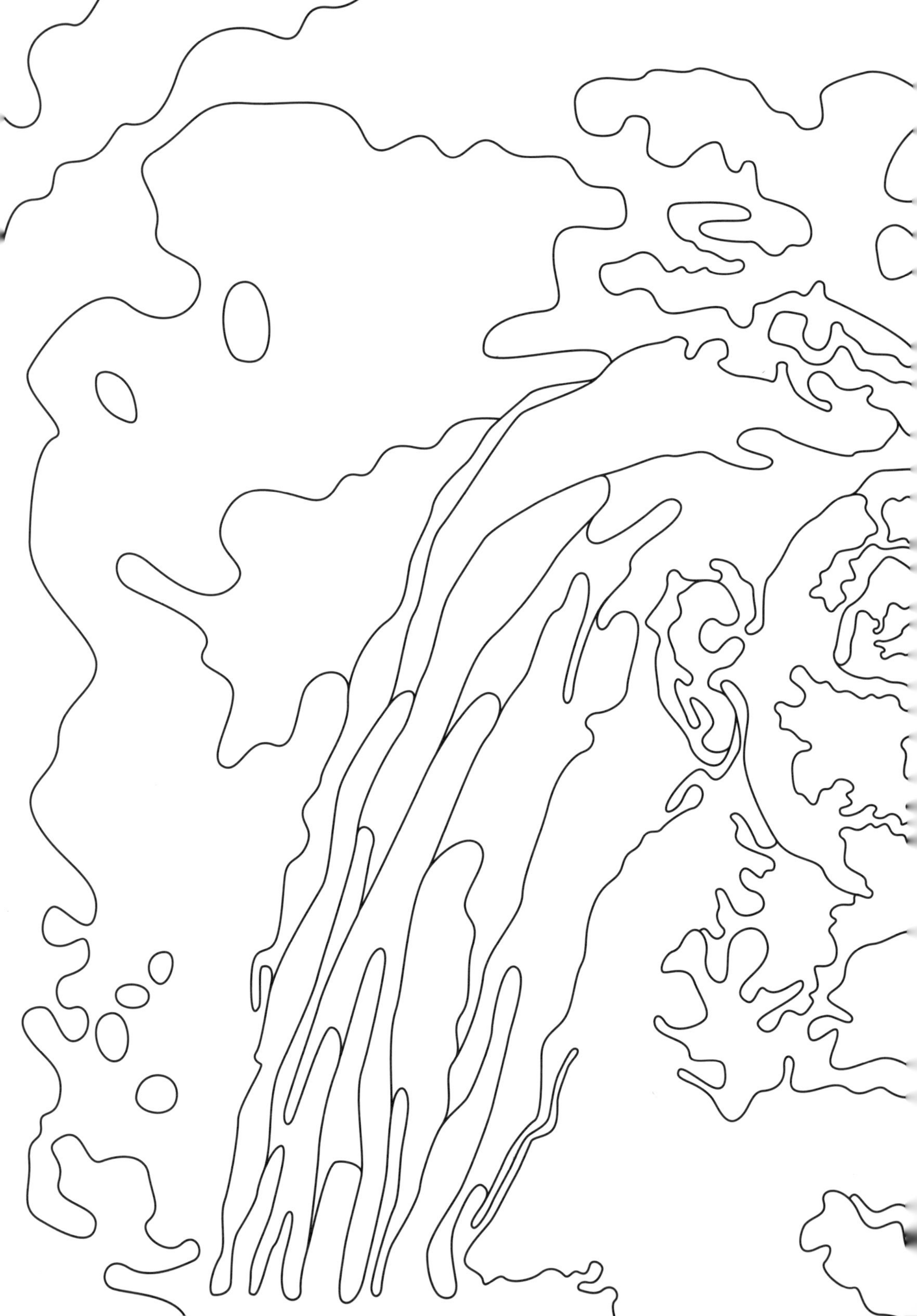

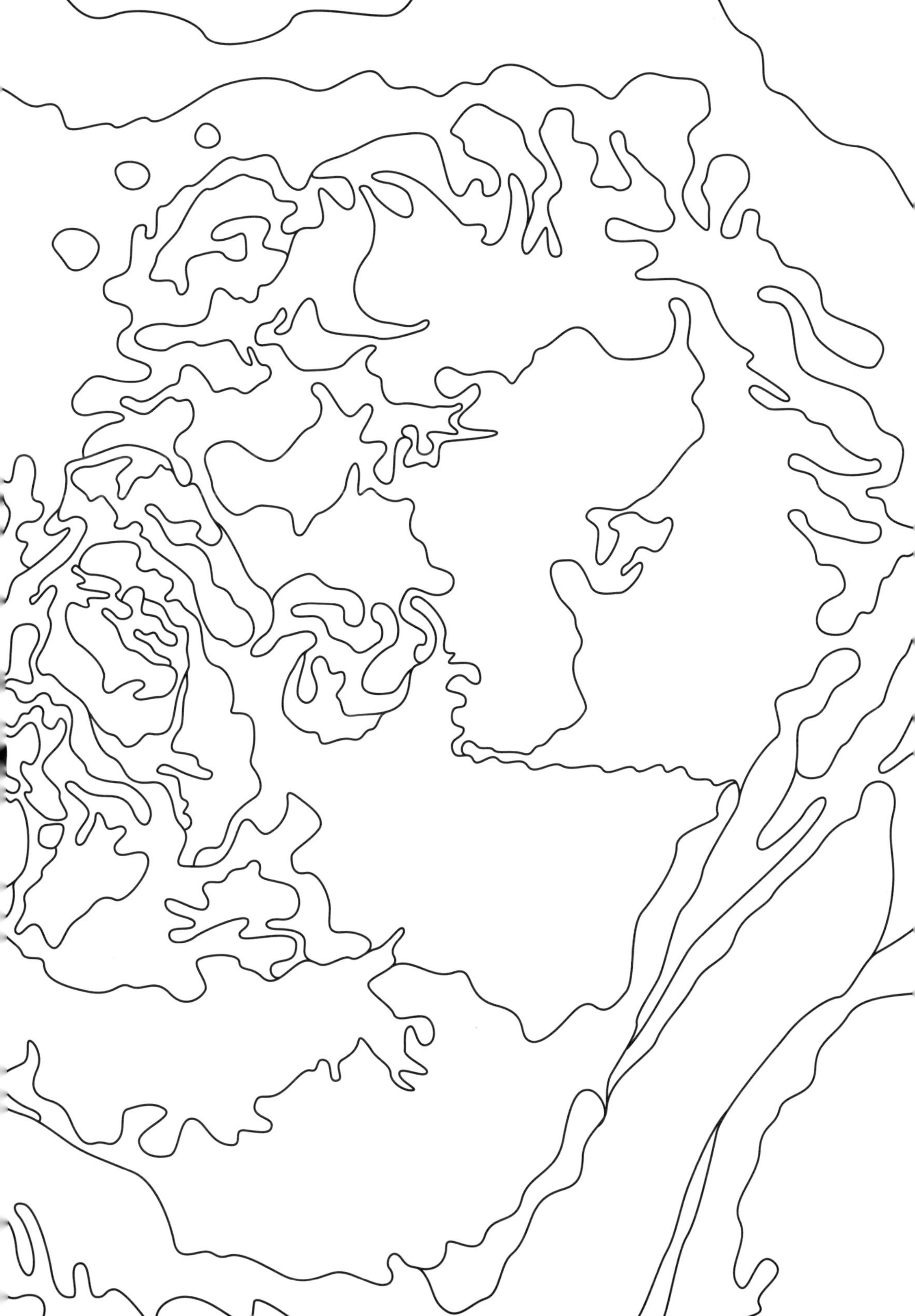

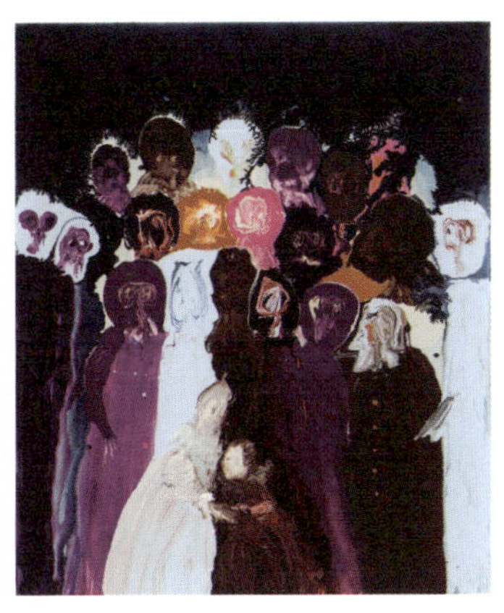

1
Crowding Around, 2016
Acrylic on canvas
47 × 39 × 1½ inches

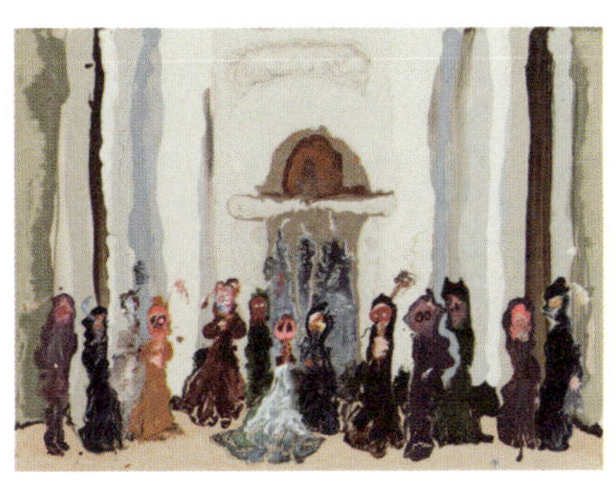

2
Masked Ball, 2016
Acrylic on wood panel
23½ × 31 inches

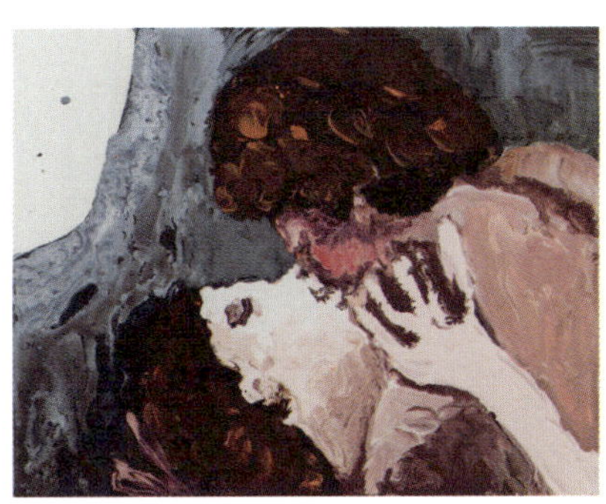

3
Kissing Under the Moon, 2016
Acrylic on wood panel
12 × 16 inches

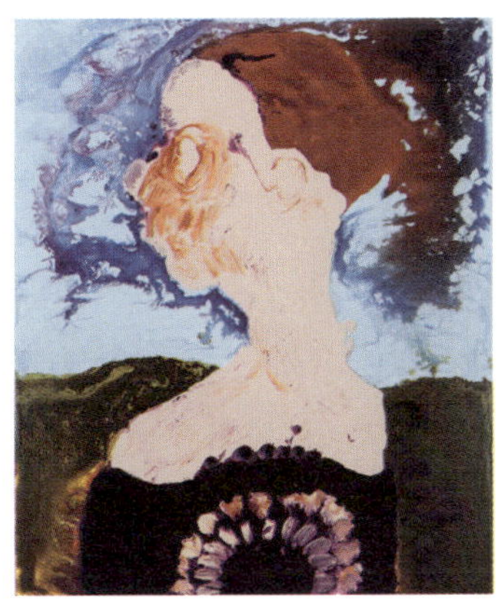

4
Portrait of a Girl, 2016
Acrylic on wood panel
24 × 20 inches

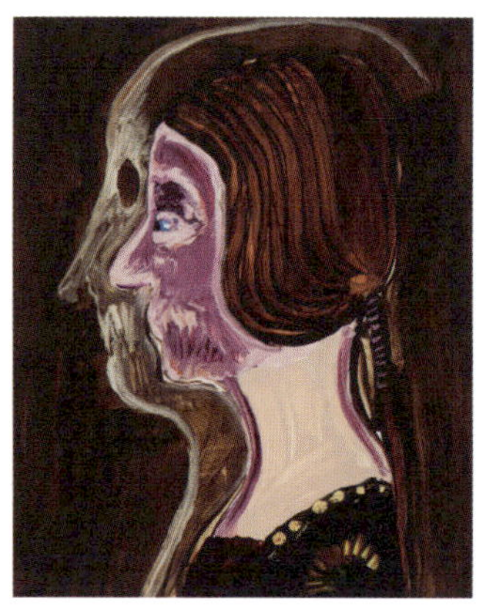

5
Juliet's Shadow, 2016
Acrylic on wood panel
12 × 9½ inches

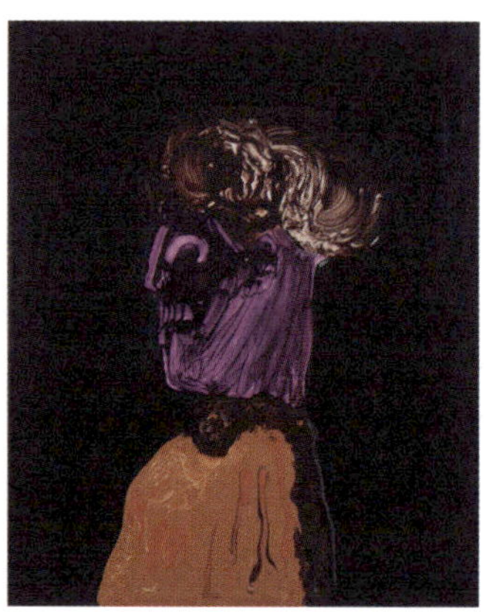

6
A Gentleman from Verona, 2016
Acrylic on wood panel
12 × 9½ inches

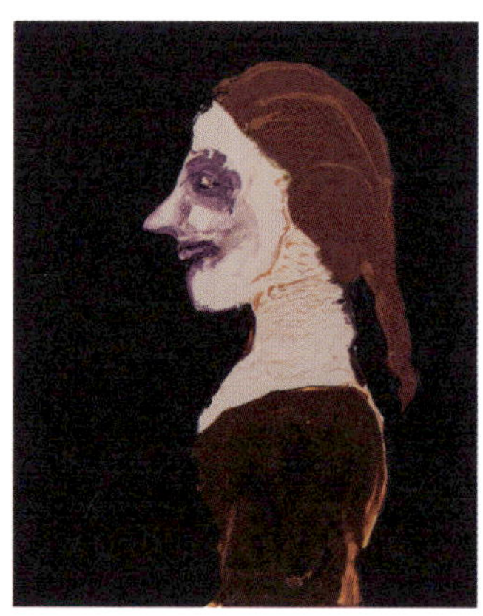

7
Juliet, 2016
Acrylic on wood panel
12 × 9½ inches

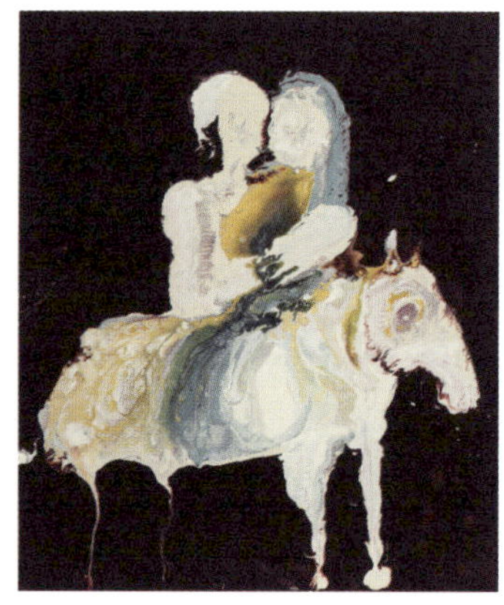

8
Romeo and Juliet on a Horse, 2016
Acrylic on canvas
47 × 39 × 2 inches

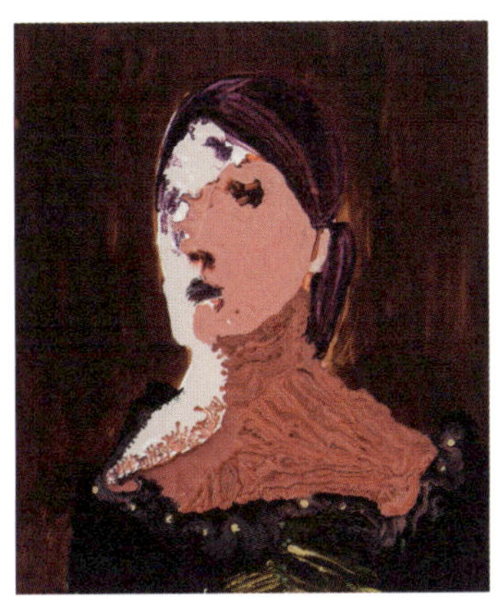

9
Portrait of a Lady from Verona, 2016
Acrylic on wood panel
23½ × 19½ inches

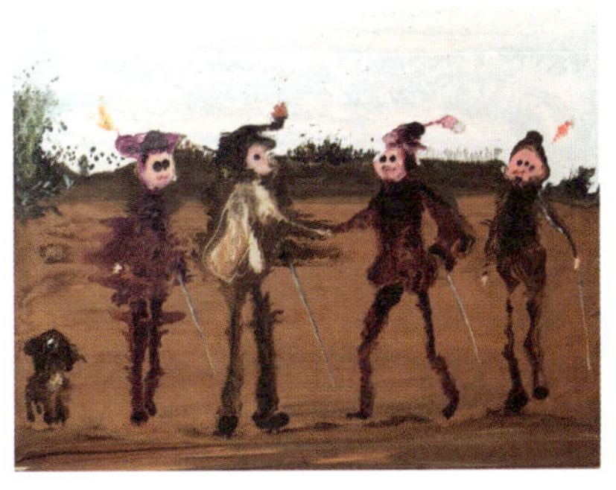

10
Gentlemen Shaking Hands, 2016
Acrylic on wood panel
12 × 19½ inches

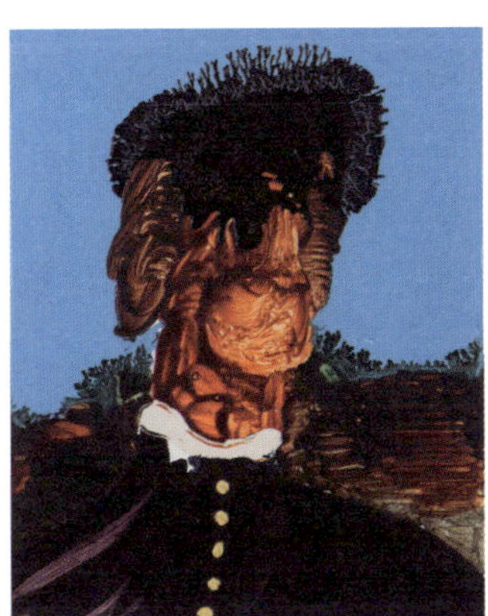

11
Man with a Purple Hat, 2016
Acrylic on wood panel
12 × 9½ inches

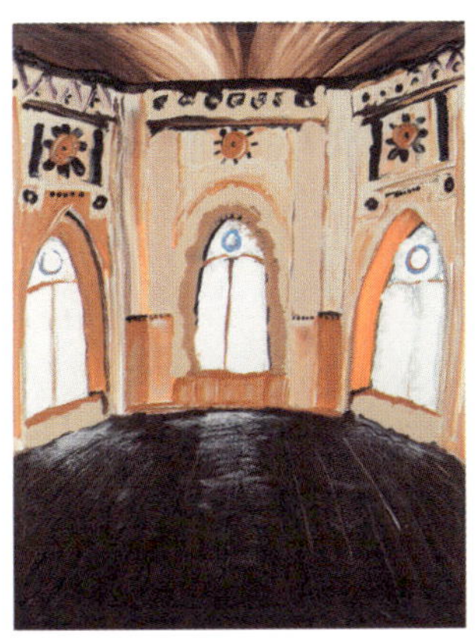

12
Room, 2016
Acrylic on wood panel
31½ × 23½ inches

13
Blue Sky Balcony, 2016
Acrylic on canvas
47 × 59 × 2 inches

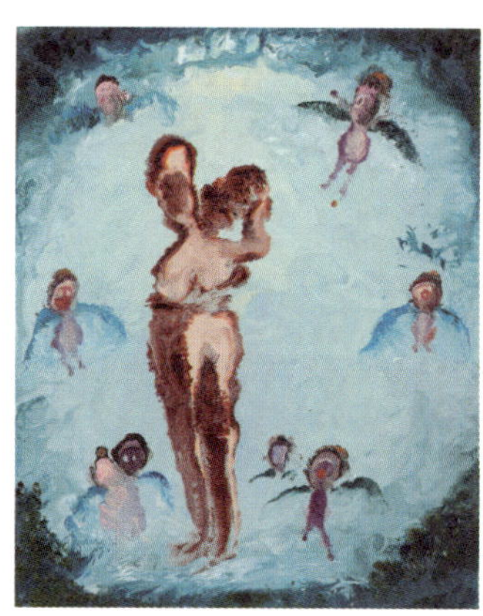

14
Ascension, 2016
Acrylic on wood panel
19½ × 16 inches

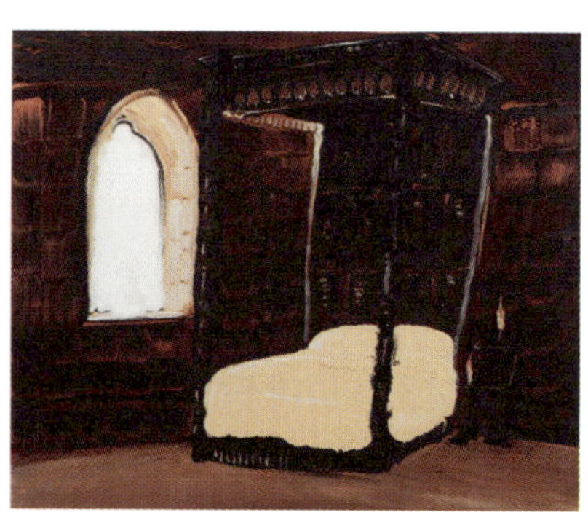

15
Bed, 2016
Acrylic on wood panel
19½ × 24 inches

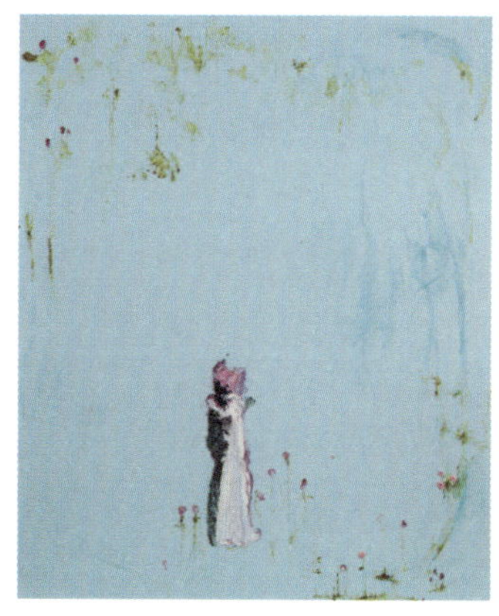

16
The Kiss, 2016
Acrylic on canvas
80 × 64½ × 2 inches

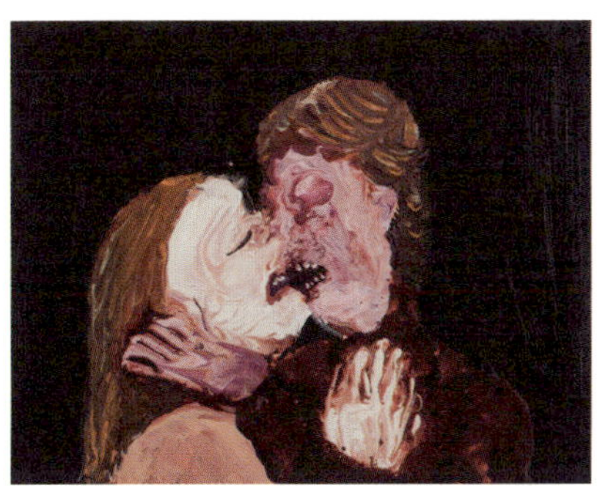

17
Eating Each Other, 2016
Acrylic on wood panel
9½ × 12 inches

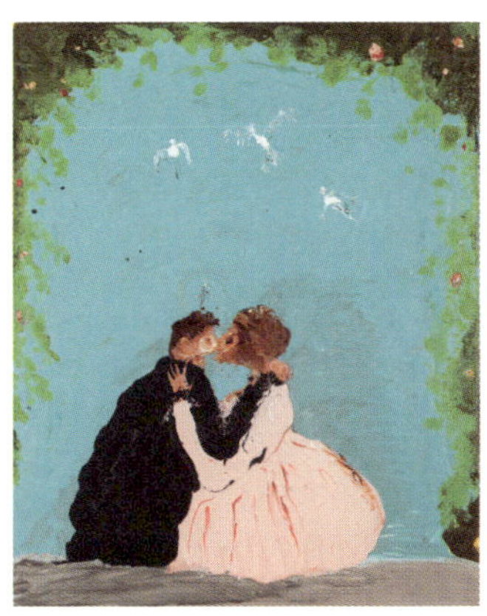

18
Kissing in the Garden, 2016
Acrylic on wood panel
19½ × 15½ inches

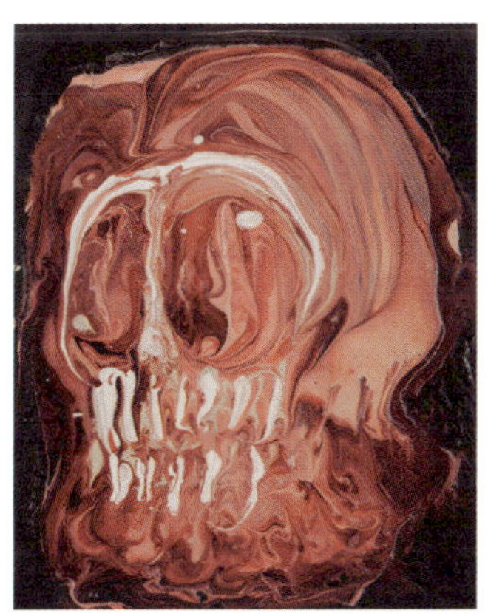

19
Skull, 2016
Acrylic on wood panel
12 × 9½ inches

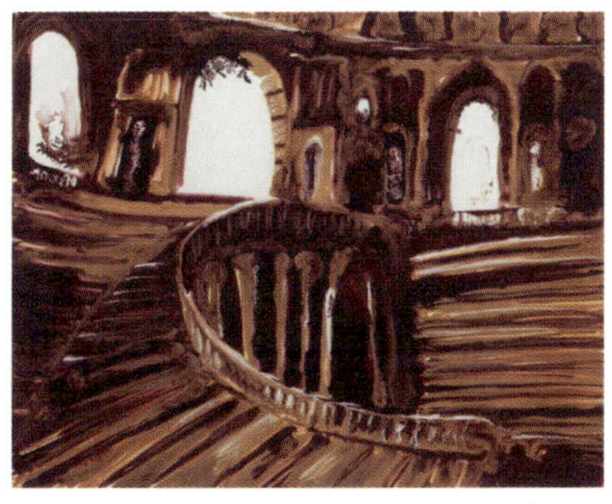

20
Staircase, 2016
Acrylic on wood panel
9½ × 12 inches

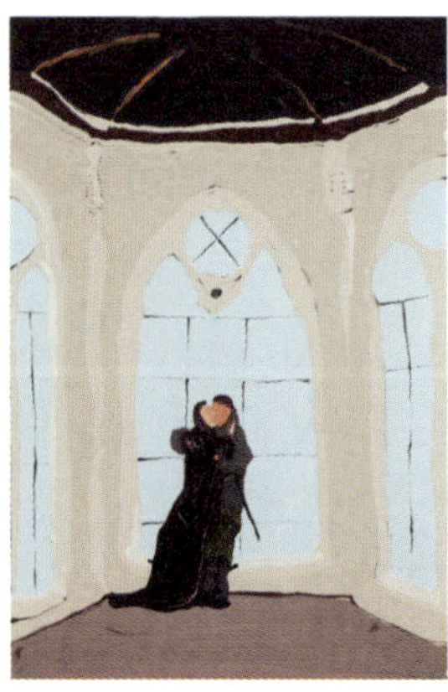

21
Kissing by the Window, 2016
Acrylic on canvas
19½ × 15½ × 1½ inches

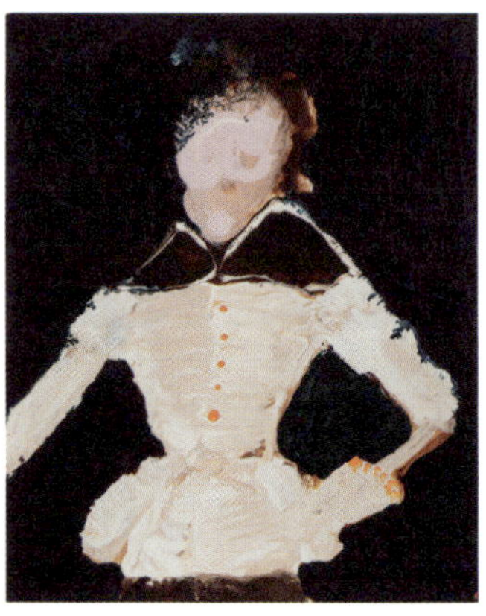

22
Romeo, 2016
Acrylic on wood panel
12 × 9½ inches

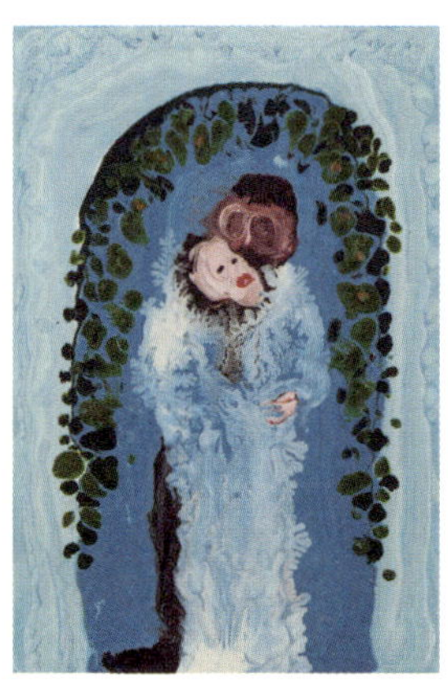

23
Garden Embrace, 2016
Acrylic on wood panel
12 × 8 inches

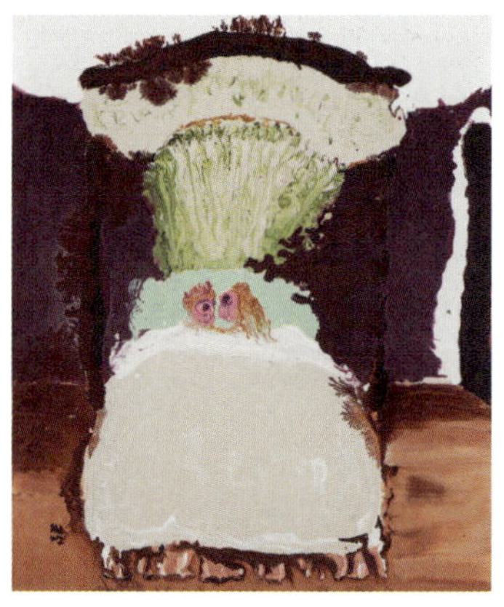

24
In Bed Together, 2016
Acrylic on canvas
47 × 39 × 1½ inches

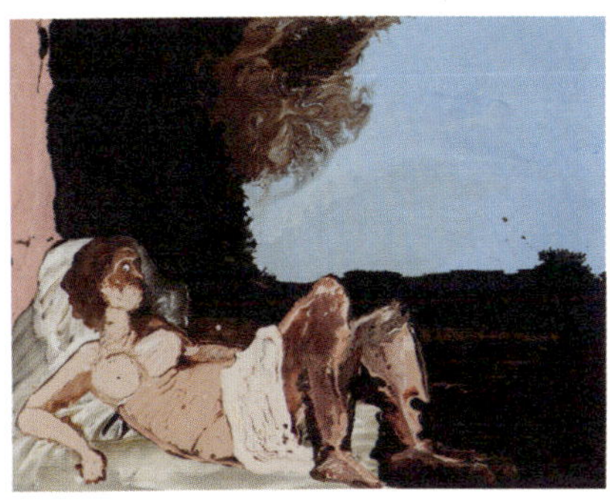

25
Waiting for My Romeo, 2016
Acrylic on canvas
31 × 39 × 2 inches

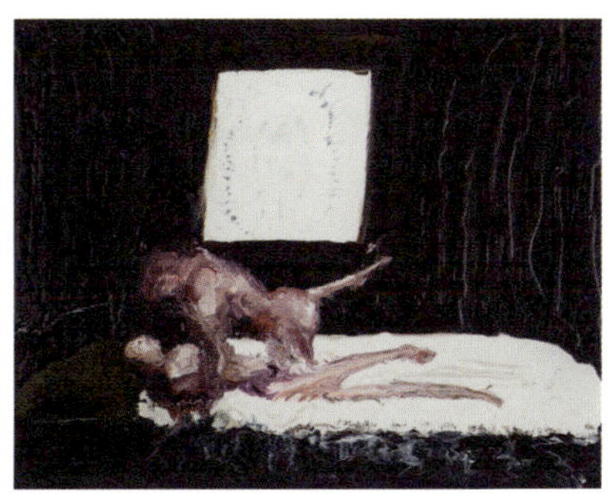

26
Bedtime, 2016
Acrylic on wood panel
15½ × 19½ inches

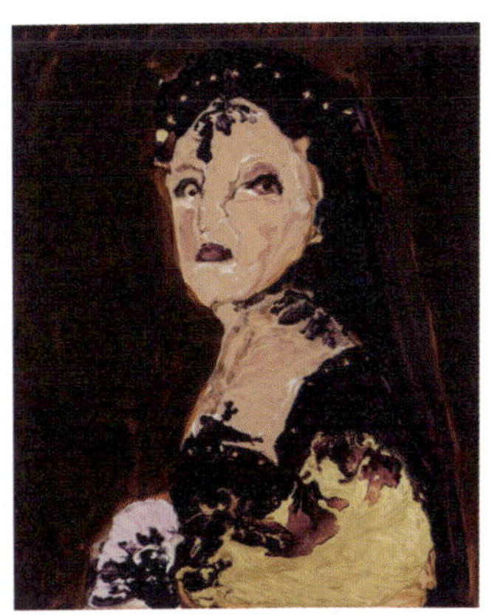

27
Mother, 2016
Acrylic on wood panel
20 × 16 inches

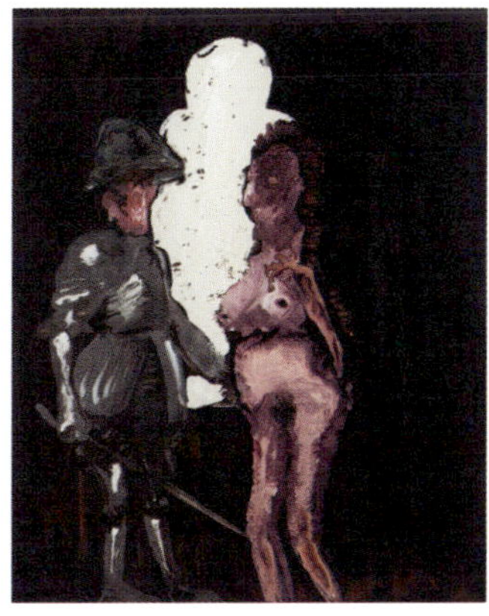

28
Where's Your Ticket Miss, 2016
Acrylic on wood panel
19½ × 15½ inches

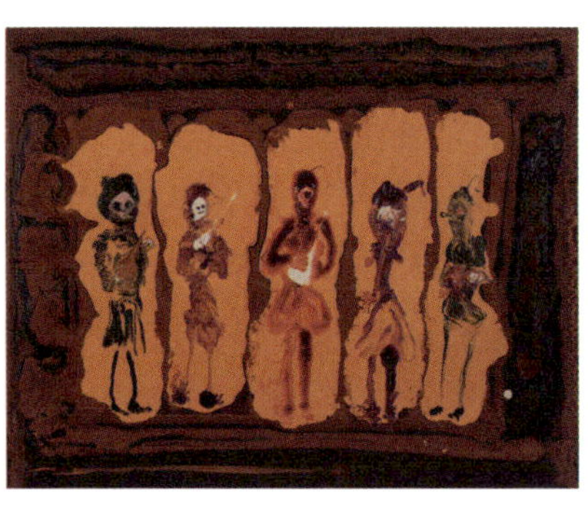

29
The Musicians, 2016
Acrylic on wood panel
15½ × 19½ inches

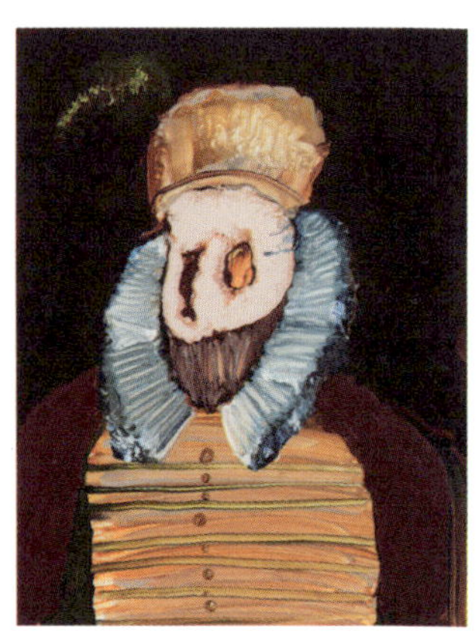

30
Gentleman with a Green Feather, 2016
Acrylic on wood panel
16 × 12 inches

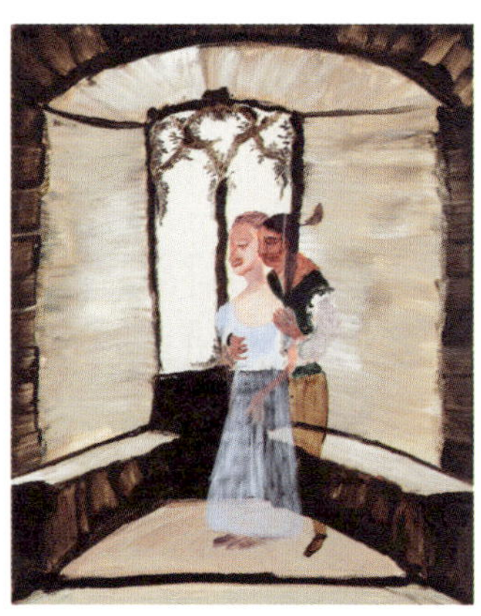

31
Ghostly Embrace, 2016
Acrylic on wood panel
19½ × 15½ inches

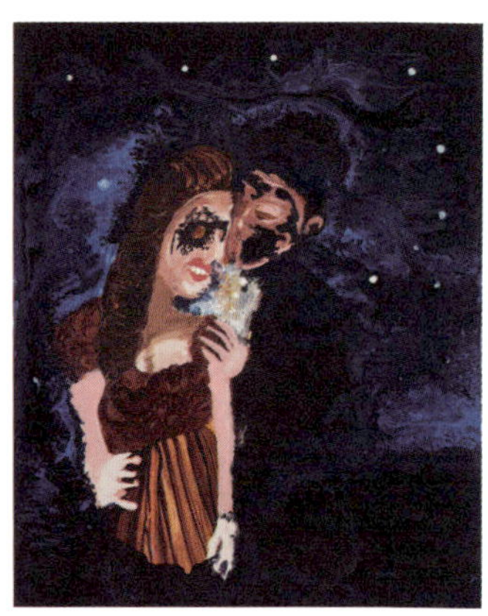

32
Masks in the Moonlight, 2016
Acrylic on wood panel
19½ × 15½ inches

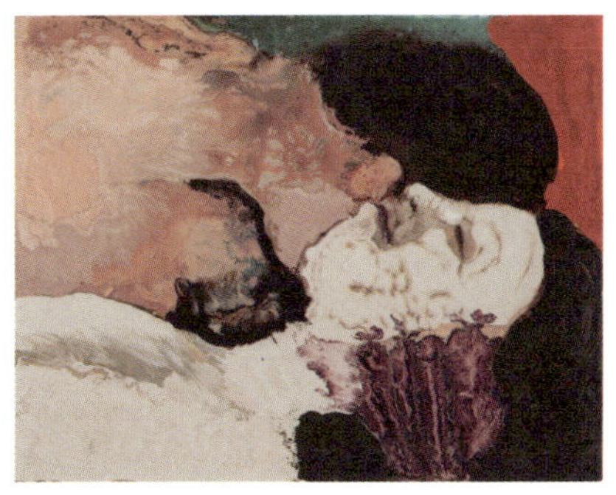

33
Don't Leave, 2016
Acrylic on wood panel
15½ × 19½ inches

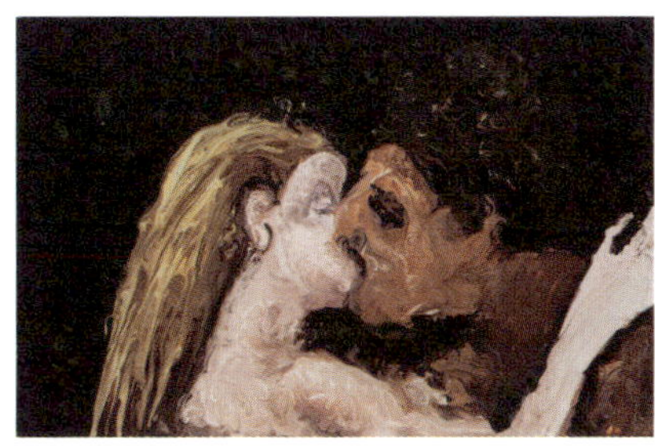

34
Juliet Kissing Her Romeo, 2016
Acrylic on wood panel
4 × 6 inches

Genieve Figgis
Something for Lovers

Published on the occasion
of her exhibition at

Gallery Met
Metropolitan Opera

December 7, 2016–
January 21, 2017

The show was organized
by Dodie Kazanjian
to coincide with the
Metropolitan Opera's new
production of *Roméo et Juliette*

Edition of 1,200

Photography: Aoife Herrity

ISBN: 978-1-942607-56-4